I0095357

COLOR SECRETS
LEARNING THE ONE UNIVERSAL LANGUAGE
WE WERE NEVER TAUGHT

MICHELLE LEWIS

To the Creator of all things, who has given us eyes to see. (1 Corinthians 2:9)

To those He's given me to love, who have helped me heal so I could see clearly.

And to those still living in grayscale: may you find your color spark within these pages & tap into your purpose using this language to guide you.

Michelle Lewis
Visibility Vixen® LLC
The Color Institute™
First Edition

Copyright © 2022 Michelle Anderson-Lewis & Visibility Vixen LLC.

Intellectual property of The Color Institute™
All rights reserved. No part of this book may be reproduced in any form, stored in any retrieval system, or transmitted in any form by any means - electronic, mechanical, photocopy, recording, or used in any manner - without the prior written permission of the copyright owner, except for the use of brief quotations in a book review.

To request permissions, contact the publisher at hello@colorinstitute.com.

Library of Congress Control Number: 2022914370
Publisher's Cataloging-in-Publication data
Names: Lewis, Michelle, author.
Title: Color secrets : learning the one universal language we were never taught / Michelle Lewis.
Description: First Edition. | Includes bibliographical references. | Hayden, ID: Michelle Lewis, 2022.
Identifiers: LCCN: 2022914370 | ISBN: 979-8-9867215-3-8 (hardcover) | 979-8-9867215-2-1 (paperback)| 979-8-9867215-1-4 (audio) | 979-8-9867215-0-7 (ebook)
Subjects: LCSH Color. | Color in design. | Color in interior decoration. | Color in marketing. | Color in nature. | Color (Philosophy) | BISAC HOUSE; HOME / General | SELF-HELP / General | LANGUAGE ARTS; DISCIPLINES / Communication Studies
Classification: LCC QC495 .L49 2022 | DDC 535--dc23

First edition published in 2022.

Edited by Tawney Anderson.
Cover design by Iren Harutyunyan.
Photograph of hand on cover ©2022 by Shutterstock
colorinstitute.com
@colorpsychologist

Disclaimers:

- This book does not replace the advice of a medical professional. Consult your physician before making any changes to your diet, health plan or regular lifestyle.
- The information in this book was correct at the time of publication, but the Author does not assume any liability for loss or damage caused by errors or omissions.
- These are observations from the Author's perspective, they have been represented as faithfully as possible.
- Color is a Universal Language™ is a protected intellectual property concept developed by Michelle Lewis under the registered trademark Visibility Vixen® (2016), published in the copyrighted book, *Color Secrets: Learning The One Universal Language We Were Never Taught* (2022), and further expanded through Color Cured™ and The Color Institute™ (2022–2025). All rights reserved under U.S. copyright and trademark law.

Citation:

Lewis, M. Color Secrets. (2022). www.colorinstitute.com.

FOREWORD

I was born blue.

Diagnosed with Hyaline Membrane Disease, where you can't produce the enzyme surfactin in order to exhale.

Growing up immune compromised has its own set of inhibitions. You can't run, or you'll need a steroid breathing treatment. If you're at school during cold or flu season, you'll always get sick and be out on antibiotics for a month. You can't play the trumpet, you just don't have the lungs. I'm sure you or a family member can easily relate.

Then, if you add severe bullying to the list, your world gets even smaller. Choked and threatened in the girls' bathroom. Threatened to be stabbed. Stress every morning to pick an outfit that wouldn't be ridiculed, but also trying to pick the right one that might get someone's attention in a positive way so they'll talk to you. That anyone - will just talk to you.

The world becomes oh, so very small.

In my early 20s, I was mostly on bed rest for two years. An exciting field trip was making it to my front door to sit on the steps in the sun. My only adventure for 600 days was sunlight. The rest was a dark room with yellow walls and a television.

I'm sharing this with you because those dark days led me to sunlight. That same sun had not only given me comfort, but given me a message. It led me to the discovery of color because, for quite some time, it was my only friend. And it is truly the one thing that has helped me heal - mind, body and spirit.

I had to figure out how it was possible. What color truly is, what it does and how it impacts the body. Then I had to prove it with science, behavioral studies and actual experiments. That's why this book exists, for you to read and experience color in your own unique way. Possibly even for your own healing on some level.

There are a lot of amazing color psychology books out there. Books have been written on color theory, color in film, color in design, color in medicine. Studies and experiments have been performed with color in every single aspect you can think of...even chickens and bees.

But no one, to my knowledge, has put it all together to create one key concept that I will be introducing you to: that color is our only universal language™. (And yes, I coined this phrase. It is now commonly used by major color companies like Pantone®.)

I've had to learn to speak it by studying its history and most importantly, how it has morphed and changed, even grown, over time. Color is more than a theory. It is a presence - something alive that changes its mediums of communication depending on its environment. Even depending on whether or not we are in the room.

It's so much cooler than science fiction. Color is science fact that will rock what you know about the world around you down to your very core.

Let me show you this new (but old as time) language that we can all use in full integrity to more effectively communicate with each other worldwide. It starts by simply standing in the sun.

SECTION ONE
UNDERSTANDING HOW WE INTERPRET COLORS

INTRODUCTION

Somewhere...over the rainbow...skies are blue.

We all heard this song growing up. And we eventually watched *The Wizard Of Oz,* where our eyes were opened to the incredible world of color. The yellow golden streets. The green skin of the wicked witch. The ruby red slippers.

For me, color has been a lifelong path of discovery that I still haven't found the end to.

Every time I try to put a period at the end of a sentence on color, it keeps going. So, naturally, I keep searching.

- How color is used in design inside of buildings, outside in city design, in art.
- How color is used by plants - which aspects of light they absorb and then reflect.
- How color is tied to the visible light spectrum - and why every color also has a frequency/sound.
- How color is used in film - how it shapes a movie from start to finish.

- How color is used by the biggest and most successful companies in the world.
- How color is used in medicine - all the uses for bringing healing to the body.
- How color is used in culture - how colors are tied to very specific and deep meanings.

On and on we go...like a never-ending carousel. I'm not sure I'll ever find the end of it. And I'm honestly not sure I want to.

There is something extremely comforting about an element that does not have a strict limit. Somehow it helps us hand over our trust - with an inner-knowing that this infinite world of color can show us something even deeper about ourselves. For a lifetime.

This book is an accumulation of years of study across every aspect of color I could think of. You'll probably find more. And I hope you'll report back. I plan on many, many more books detailing every aspect of color in the future.

There are eleven basic terms for color in the English language: red, yellow, green, blue, purple, orange, pink, gray, white, brown and black. We'll talk about the seven that create an actual response in the body and the four that don't for the most part.

I'll show you...

- Why you love certain interior designers on *HGTV*
- Why that vacation to Spain left an unquenchable desire to return
- What color you should wear to your family reunion
- That you painted your bedroom the worst color imaginable
- How your personality can change

My goal with this book is to show you how using color as a language can impact and forever change your life in every facet.

THE UNIVERSAL LANGUAGE OF COLOR™

A LANGUAGE IS DEFINED as "the words, their pronunciation, and the methods of combining them used and understood by a community". - *Merriam-Webster*

Whenever a group of people come together with a method of communication that has a specific structure, a language is formed.

I'm not inventing a language here, but I am proposing that we officially classify color as a universal language. This would be the first time in history one language could be defined as being spoken by every person on earth no matter their location.

I propose color as a universal language because we can all speak it once it's learned. Color can cross divides like other languages, cultures, genders and generations.

"The limits of my language mean the limits of my world". - *Ludwig Wittgenstein, philosopher*

As I've gotten more and more obsessed with color, I've found its effects to be undeniable and universal. It may not

mean the same exact thing in every culture worldwide, especially throughout history, but as humans...we always react to it.

Whenever I teach a class for a colleague's audience, I never
immediately thrust color meaning into their reality. That's an
old teaching style. I simply show the colors in the visible light
spectrum, adding pink and magenta (you'll learn why later),
and ask for their gut reaction.

No one has ever said they have no reaction. Ever. I've seen
joy, anger, sadness, reflection, peace, connection, laughter -
even grief. But never 'nothing'.

That tells me, along with a never-ending stack of scientific
evidence, that color has been grossly, horribly underestimated.

Not by the toy companies. Or by the pharmaceutical industries. Not even by fast food chains. It's been underestimated
and even ignored by most schools, colleges, hospitals - pretty
much any institution for the most part. Fortunately, that is
starting to change.

We study foreign languages in efforts to communicate. I
would strongly say that by learning color, we could communicate on an even greater scale anywhere in the world by helping
people do one thing...*feel*.

> "If you talk to a man in a language he understands, that goes
> to his head. If you talk to him in his language, that goes to his
> heart." - Nelson Mandela, activist

That's why my goal in life is to teach this language. Making
it a second language we all can become fluent in, so we can
truly speak with each other and effectively communicate. As
we learn to speak color, we will start combining all aspects of
ourselves (mental, physical, emotional, spiritual) within our
communication.

For example, I think about how my life would have been

impacted if my parents would have known this language as I endured years of violent bullying in middle school. Would blue have made me feel more peaceful? Would orange have been the best color in my room because it felt safe and homey? Would wearing green to school have helped students respond to me in a different way?

Then I think about college when my physical issues became insurmountable and I spent a few years on bed rest. Could I have put certain colors on my body or in my room to support my healing? Was black clothing something I hid behind that contributed to my organs shutting down because I spent all of my time inside with nothing in the visible light spectrum for my body to absorb?

Looking back, I'd say unequivocally - yes!

Now I can use what I've learned to support your journey into learning this universal language. The only one that can be found simply by looking at the sun. The only language that can actually be worn. The only universal language that is proven to impact the body, the mind, the emotions...even history, politics and wars.

I've studied color in medicine, color in film, color in design, color in nature, color in human bodies, color in the visible light spectrum, color in science, even color in the brain. And it bridges every gap, every topic, every discovery and every culture.

- A new medicine? The chemical compounds dilute down into one primary color.
- A music note? The frequency correlates to a specific color in the visible light spectrum.
- A certain fruit or vegetable? Foods that contain specific nutrients that reflect as a certain light pigment.

- Lasers used in hospitals, space and engineering?
  Yep. Specific colors there too that determine power
  and potency.

It's wild. And it's wonderful. All at the same time.

And if I can do one thing in my color career...it would be to simply bring awareness of the connection of this universal language to as many people as I can.

Let's start with you.

"One language sets you in a corridor for life. Two languages open every door along the way." - Frank Smith, psycholinguist

COLOR & THE BRAIN

WE ARE BORN into a blurry world. As infants, we don't see color until we're about 2-4 months old. By 5 months, we see most colors and can easily distinguish between red, yellow, green and blue.

Let's start with the basics of how this happens. The *retina* is a part of our eye that receives light. It's in the very back of the eye and covers about 65% of it.

In the retina are *photoreceptors* called *rods* and *cones*. The *rods* help us with low-light vision (night vision) and the *cones* higher levels of light (color vision).

There are three types of cones that help us differentiate colors. The first helps us see long waves of light, which translates to reds. The second helps us see shorter wavelengths of light, which translates to blues. And lastly, a cone for in-between waves such as greens.

Our cones trigger the release of a chemical transmitter which initiates an electrical signal that the occipital lobe of the brain - specifically the *visual cortex* - interprets. This completes the loop when you see a tree leaf, for example, your cones pick up the shade of color, send it to the brain and you think "green".

But it doesn't stop there.

The visual cortex isn't the only piece of the brain that receives the information. The *hypothalamus* (linking your endocrine system and nervous system) and the *pituitary gland* (which makes essential hormones) absorb the information too.

This governs pretty much everything. Sleep, appetite, the autonomous nervous system, water regulation and even our metabolism.

These parts of the brain use information about light to cause a reaction in the body. Our eyes start to see light in the morning - the brain starts sending hormones like *cortisol* to wake us up. The sun starts to set - *melatonin* is released to make us sleepy.

Remember the green leaf? Let's keep going with this new information. We've established that so far the brain makes you think "green" when you see this leaf. Let's now send this information to the hypothalamus and pituitary gland. Your body will have a reaction now. Possibly relaxation because of associating this color with nature and taking a deep breath in order to inhale the essential oils being dispersed from the trees. (Proven by a Japanese study referenced at the end of this book that we activate NK cells and anti-cancer proteins after visiting a forest - the effect of which lasts for seven days.)

Am I being clear here? Light, which our brain interprets as colors, not only is seen by the brain as information, but also as the governance of its daily operation.

We can see a range of approximately 17 million colors, which means our bodies can have potentially 17 million reactions. Absolutely mind-blowing, right?

Okay. So we've figured out how the brain interprets color and how that affects our responses. But I need to know one more thing. Where does the brain categorically code color?

I was first able to find a study that proved through MRI scans that learning new names for colors increases the gray matter of the brain in the *left visual cortex*, a region that mediates color vision. They even found changes in the *cerebellum*! (See the 2011 PNAS study at the back of this book.) That means you can look up these colors as we go through them in the book and know that you're building brain matter!

Going even deeper, another study removed all stumbling blocks of brain color coding, like language barriers, to do in-depth fMRI scans and they found something even more mind-blowing. There was an undeniable effect of color category in 3 brain regions: the left and right *middle frontal gyrus* (MFG), and the *left cerebellum*. (2014 Stanford study, bibliography)

If you take your hands, make them flat like a robot, and line your thumbs against your eyebrows...straight back on either side...that's your MFG. The MFG do more categorical processing in terms of phonetics, dot patterns, spatial memory. It's a very general categorical storage system for the brain. The cerebellum is at the very base of your skull. It's most associated with motor coordination.

Color processing and storage in the brain is still very much unknown and undefined. Modern science has studies that show truths as we've seen here...but a lot of it is still a mystery.

Here is tangible proof that more of our brain is involved with color than just coming up with the name. We've seen how it actually codes it in different ways throughout the brain - crossing barriers where we store language, information, motor function, memory and processing centers.

So what did we really prove here? That the brain indeed

sees color as a language, but with much more power than a language simply comprised of words.

Our brains involve aspects of our body, mind and emotions when processing and communicating with color. Proving effectively that color is the most powerful language when it comes to the brain and the body.

COLOR PHYSICS
IS COLOR PARTICLE OR WAVE?

It's easy to simply list the different aspects of color and how they're perceived. What I'm asking you to do, however, is much more complicated.

I'm asking you to accept color as the universal language of humans throughout history and today. A pretty monumental ask.

It's not enough to talk film, culture and history. I have to bring to you the scientific and physics-backed studies on light as it's the basis of what we see.

We may not understand certain colors on a cultural or even natural level, but we all understand color on a physics level. Let me explain.

The first fundamental understanding of color happened with Isaac Newton in the 17th century. He proved that objects weren't innately colored as previously believed by most Greek philosophers. Instead, by using an uncolored glass prism, he showed that light going through it dispersed into seven colors: red, orange, yellow, blue, green, indigo and violet.

Think of the rainbow. Inside of a true rainbow, you will see these colors in this exact order, from the top down.

Newton proved no other colors existed by putting another prism behind the first. The seven colors reverted back to white when passing through the second prism. Essentially? Newton helped us understand that sunlight creates seven colors we can see in everything.

So how do we differentiate between the seven colors and all of their shades? That is done by wavelength.

We see what is termed the *visible light spectrum*, which ranges from 380-740 nanometers or 405-790 terahertz. This defines the light we can see.

Many more wavelengths exist in the electromagnetic spectrum of our world, however. There are - from bottom to top - *long radio waves, FM/AM broadcast bands, short radio waves, infrared waves, visible light spectrum waves, ultraviolet waves, x-ray waves* and *gamma rays.*

Making sense so far? The frequencies in our world range from long radio waves to gamma rays. The only ones we can actually see, however, are within the visible light spectrum. These are the seven colors of the rainbow.

Accepting light as both a *particle* (a minute portion of matter) and a *wave* is crucial to understanding how we are all affected by color and can utilize it in communication, like its own language.

In 1801, physicist and ophthalmologist Thomas Yong developed the *double-slit experiment.* He wanted to see if light behaved as a particle or a wave, as previous scientists believed one or the other. Here's the weird part. As the experiment commenced, light acted as both, but it was entirely dependent on whether or not it was being observed. This is called *The Observer's Effect.* As light passed through the two slits of the experiment, it behaved as waves when not observed and particles when observed.

This is really hard to fully comprehend, even for top scientists and physicists, so don't stress if it takes a few reads to get a basic grasp here.

Yong's experiment proved that light acted as both. The only variable to what light appeared as was whether or not a person was there watching.

If light was alone, it behaved as a *wave* - energy. If someone was there, it behaved as a *particle* - matter.

Stay with me. We need to understand one more crucial thing.

In 1929, Louis de Broglie won the Nobel Prize for officially uniting the two theories that light is both wave and particle. Termed *matter waves*, Broglie's theory was instrumental to the forward momentum of physics as it finally explained why electrons (negative charged particles inside an atom) are limited in their restricted motion around the nucleus of an atom. The idea of the electron also containing the properties of a wave explained the mystery, as a wave confirmed within the boundaries imposed by a nuclear charge would restrict its shape.

This proved electrons had not only *corpuscular* (little particle) properties, but also could behave as *radiant energy*. For me, it helped explain the incredible observer's effect in Yong's experiment. By adding ourselves to the atmosphere of the experiment, it would have also added an additional electromagnetic field, possibly contributing to light behaving as a particle.

Because light was in close proximity to a particle-based, electromagnetic being giving off its own magnetic field...the light not only recognized, but adjusted its composition to mimic and relate to the being.

If we take this to its logical conclusion, light will adjust itself to us in an effort to communicate (from wave to particle) when we enter its atmosphere. It will likely react in specific ways. I'd even dare say our particles, when coming into contact with its particles, will absorb and reflect according to what light particles we need in our hormone manufacturing. (This theory is the basis for Color Analysis.)

Granted, this is my personal conclusion. But it helped me understand how much further light, and therefore color, is truly related to us as physical, electromagnetic beings and how we respond to it. Color isn't just a frequency of light we see in objects. It is a particle that is comprised in the very atoms of our physical matter.

Let me prove to you that we are in fact *electromagnetic beings* that could cause this reaction.

We are electric beings because electricity is essential to our operation.

The elements within our bodies (sodium, potassium, calcium, magnesium) carry specific electrical charges that our cells use to generate electricity. Even our cell membranes function so our cells can generate electrical currents. We also have negative and positive charges that our cells use to create certain behaviors; like positive charges that turn electrical currents into electrical pulses or *action potentials*. This essentially causes us to move, think and behave in certain ways. Each cell has a trans-membrane potential of about 80-100 millivolts.

Think of it like our heart. Doctors can observe electrical pulses in our hearts using an electrocardiogram or ECG, right? And if the current is off, it can cause our hearts to beat incorrectly.

In addition, we are magnetic beings as well since cellular electrical activity creates small magnetic fields. Think of how they measure brain waves. They're actually measuring the brain's magnetic field using either an *magnetoencephalography* (MEG) or *electroencephalography*. (When magnetic fields are created by living things, it is called *biomagnetism*.)

So we fully understand now how much we function very similarly to light. Being comprised of electricity and magnetism. Both particle and wave.

Maybe that's why we instinctively dress according to the wave aspect of light. We put on dark clothes in the winter that absorb light and make us warmer, and lighter clothes in the summer that reflect light and keep us cooler.

This mystery is what brought in the profession of *quantum mechanics*, the science of how matter and light behave on the atomic and subatomic scale. And this unique particle of light is named a *photon* which encapsulates light, radio waves and electromagnetic waves.

Photons vibrate. And this is what helps us understand how something like light can also be measured in frequency and vibration.

Since photons encapsulates light, and light has seven visible light spectrum colors, and we can measure both the *nanometers* (wavelengths) and *terahertz* (frequency) of each color...

...we have proof to explain the physical power of color in terms of light, frequency, particles and vibration spanning hundreds of years of experiments in one chapter.

What do you think? A ton of technical, scientific terms to help prove what you knew instinctively when you picked up this book.

- That color is a communicative medium, whether it be through light, frequency, wavelength, particles or vibration. And that the massive scale of communication that color carries might easily prove that we, as humans, use this medium everyday to communicate subconsciously.

- That color is its own language that we all speak, whether we realize it or not.

THE EIGHT COLORS OF COLOR LANGUAGE

In the following section of *Color Secrets*, I am going to show you the eight primary communication colors that comprise this language.

Six exist in the visible light spectrum, two do not.

Within the visible light spectrum are the colors we see as human beings that are created by our brain's interpretation of visual wavelengths. As you've read in the *Color Physics* chapter, there are many more wavelengths we cannot see, like ultraviolet rays or infrared waves.

The seven colors we see in the visible light spectrum, like the rainbow, are:

- Red
- Orange
- Yellow
- Green
- Blue
- Indigo
- Violet

Two colors that I am adding to our color communication palette are:

- Pink
- Magenta

I will explain why I have added these two colors in detail as we progress, and why I combine blue and indigo, but for now, know this. These colors all have documented and scientifically proven responses in humans: either physically, emotionally, mentally, or a combination of the three.

Colors you do not see listed here simply don't. They can be used, of course, but they will not create the reactions in the brain or behavior like the eight I have meticulously chosen based on what I can prove.

Ready to learn the eight colors that form the Universal Language of Color™?

SECTION TWO
BREAKDOWN OF COMMUNICATION COLORS

INTRODUCING
COMMUNICATION COLORS

You may be thinking...there are a ton of color psychology experts out there. Why should I listen to this one?

I'm glad you asked because I honestly want to prove why I have such a different view on color then most people, even other color specialists.

When I was trying to figure out how to decipher the language of color, I had just started my own business. It launched to no sales, no attention, no followers, nothing.

I blamed myself. My messaging had to have been off. My design must have been terrible. It had to be me. But then I saw a book on my shelf I had gotten as a gift in film school. It was called *If It's Purple, Someone's Gunna Die*. It was all about color psychology and how it was used in film.

That made me wonder if implementing similar methods into my brand would affect an audience the same way it would if it were a movie. The relaunch went much better and worked really well, but I didn't feel like I had truly mastered understanding color enough to defend the stark change in audience response.

I further studied color in design, getting my certification in interior design. That showed me the power of color throughout history in architecture and homes, but there was no 'guide' on how to select the right colors and tones that were proven to benefit a family or a community.

That led me to studying color in healing. Figuring out how plants absorbed certain light spectrum colors to provide support or change to the body. This helped me understand that the body has actual metabolic responses when interacting with light.

(I've since also gotten a certification in Color Analysis - matching certain color families to skin tones and studied Color Theory and Color Methodologies at UCLA. I'm currently in process of earning my EMBA.)

There it was. A film degree, design and healing certifications all pointing to small pieces of a larger concept.

That color was the key to our communication.

That's why this book exists.

I've spent the last five years studying every dimension of color I could think of.

Film, science, history, culture, religion, nature, healing, music, behavior, wardrobe, branding, marketing, advertising, politics and education.

Because these are some of the aspects of color that could prove how multi-dimensionally color was involved in the very tapestry of our existence. Each piece helps put together this massive puzzle that is our color language.

As I break down each of what I like to call the primary colors of the *Universal Language Of Color™*, you'll see why the chapters are broken down as they are so you can fully grasp the concept.

RED
THE COLOR OF ATTENTION & PASSION

Of all the colors I teach, people always, always, have the best understanding of what red means on an instinctual level. Which makes sense given that it's a psychological primary that resonates with us on a physical level.

What do you think red means? Make some notes here before you read further to see what you innately know. You'll be shocked how accurate you are on at least one of the meanings of red based on your life experience.

Did you ever bring your teacher a red apple? Or get pegged with that rubber red ball during a heated dodgeball game at recess?

Were you known for your red lipstick? Or that red power tie at work?

Have you ever wondered why red cars get more speeding tickets? Or why the TEDx stage is always a red circle?

Red is the color that most says: DO SOMETHING.

This color makes us act and react. We come to a screeching halt at an intersection. We stop to grab to-go food on a road trip. We run. We lust. We do something. Instinct plays a huge role in how we interpret and act when we see red.

Maybe it's because it lies on the longest wavelength in the visible light spectrum. We see it first and it grabs our attention.

There are so many reasons why we have a behavioral response to red. We'll go over some of them in detail here because I want to prove why this is a key component of color being its own language.

SCIENCE

Red is the first color we see in the visible light spectrum. If you're looking at a rainbow, for example, it's always the top color.

It has a dominant wavelength of 625-740 nanometers. Right past that is infrared light.

There are three color models:

- RYB (red, yellow, blue - the most commonly accepted color model, used in paint)
- CMY (cyan, magenta, yellow - used in printing)
- RGB (red, green, blue - used in TVs and computers)

The RGB color model stands for 'red, green, blue' which is an additive color model where these three colors can be mixed to form any other color. Basically, this is the model we get color hex codes from that we use on TVs, computers, or even our websites.

The CMY and RGB models agree that the complimentary

color to red is cyan, which is a more blue-green color. RYB clearly states that it's green.

The visible light spectrum is a bit easier to understand when you think about sunrises and sunsets. When the sun is furthest away from our eye, we see the longest spectrum of light. Which is why we see the blues and yellows of the sky during the day, and then longer wavelengths of the oranges and reds at sunrise and sunset.

Red is the first color humans see after black and white. It's also the first color babies see. And when someone has had a traumatic brain injury that gives them temporary color blindness, red is the first color they start to see again.

In 1942, a Russian Scientist named SV Krakov conducted a study to figure out if our bodies had a tangible, physical reaction to color. He would put people in front of a blue light and measure their pulse, blood pressure and pupil dilation. After noting a reduction in stress levels after looking at blue, he tried red. Red increased blood pressure, shot up the heart rate and caused the pupils to dilate.

There was a measurable, physical reaction of stimulating the fight or flight response in our bodies when seeing red. Isn't that fascinating? Other scientific experiments involving human reaction have shown that red demonstratively strengthened motor reactions when viewed right before a task.

Let's talk about red hair. Surprisingly complicated, that's for sure. Only in 2019 did scientists get to the root cause of the color. On a very basic level, our hair color is determined by two types of melanin pigments: eumelanin (dark) and pheomelanin (light). If you have a darker hair color and skin tone that tans easily, you produce more eumelanin. If you have lighter hair and lighter skin tone, you produce more pheomelanin.

But there's a traffic cop, otherwise known as a MC1R gene, that tells the hair how much pigment to produce and what kind. It's called an 'MSH' signal. People with red hair, or 'red heads', have a variation in their MC1R gene from both parents (called polymorphism) that creates little to no eumelanin. It stimulates the production of red pigmented hair as a result.

Here's what's weird. Even in people with the MC1R gene variation from both parents, they don't always have red hair.

Dr. Ian Jackson, who supervised the study on red heads, wanted to figure out why. He studied over 343,000 cases in the UK. He and his team found 8 other genes that affected red hair coloring. Genes that controlled hair shape and texture even affected the outcome of red hair. Clearly, having red hair is a genetic miracle!

Experiments have used red to make people hungry, since it stimulates the blood pressure and heart rate. Naturally, the food market wants a way to attract us to red foods, especially artificial foods. Think candies, chips, sodas, etc. Today, the most common synthetic food dye we have is Red AC, which is mainly sourced from petroleum.

HISTORY

Let's dive into red's history used throughout world cultures.

Most cave drawings found across cultures were drawn with red "paint", taken from red ochre clays or cinnabar. The oldest rumored discovery lies in a cave in South Africa, 40,000-170,000 years ago.

These caves were painted by Stone Age hunters and gatherers, who used red clay to make body paint. They also used this red powder when burying their dead, supposedly to ward off evil spirits.

Spain found a painting of a red bison painted with red

ochre dating back to 16,500-15,000 BC. In Northern Australia, there is a rock art site called Djulirri that has a red painting of a thylacoleo dating back to 11,000 BCE. Over 11,000 paintings are stretched over the site.

Ancient Egyptians used red pigment to color their bodies for celebrations and victories. And the roots of the madder plant were used for many, many years to create red dye.

In ancient Rome, red was associated with the god of Mars or the god of war. The planet Mars was named after him because of its color. At weddings of this time period, brides wore red shawls, symbolizing love and fidelity. China carries on the tradition to this day.

The Romans used red pigment from the mineral cinnabar to create their bright shade of red, called vermillion. This pigment was actually, in itself, highly toxic mercury. (Now we know why slaves and prisoners did the mining work in the Southern Spanish mines to source the material.)

China holds very prosperous ties to the color red since it's one of their five elemental colors. The Jin, Ming, Song, Han and Zhou dynasties all favored the color for their emperors. In a painting of the Tang-Era, eleven of the thirteen Emperors are in red robes. The Han Dynasty also used lead tetroxide for their red pigments between 200 BC - 200 AD.

In the 1500s, the Spaniards discovered an amazing shade of red being made by the Aztecs. They would crush cochineal bugs off of cacti, creating shades like kermes. This became their new hot commodity to trade to Europe, which became immensely popular.

Red is most seen and celebrated as an artistic color in Renaissance and Baroque art. What's really interesting is that their favorite color red, coined red lac, was actually made organically - using plants, insects, chalk, or trees. You can see the ties between red and royalty with *The Assumption*, a painting by Titian which shows God, the Virgin Mary and two apostles in vermillion colored robes.

The young Princess Elizabeth I showed her preparation for becoming Queen by sitting for a portrait dressed in red. This signaled to the nation her intention of strength. Revolutionaries worldwide followed suit, using red to symbolize their quest for freedom, like with the French Revolution and Cuban Revolution. In the middle ages, the Pope and Cardinals of the Roman Catholic Church wore red to symbolize the blood of Christ and the Christian martyrs.

In 1868, German Chemists found a way to synthetically create red dye, calling it Alizarin, which became its permanent replacement.

Red is one of the key colors used throughout history and one of our foundational communication colors worldwide.

CURRENT CULTURE & RELIGION

Red is used today in a variety of cultures and religions.

In Buddhism, it's seen as one of the colors of enlightenment. In Japan, it symbolizes moving from the profane world into a sacred space.

Red is a common color for uniforms in sports and competitions. There is all kinds of fascinating research that proves that referees have a bias towards red, so teams with that colored uniform have historically higher victory counts.

It is seen as the Republican party color in the United States.

The color red is very sacred in China. Not only is it the color of their country's flag, but it represents one of their sacred colors relating to fire, symbolizing good fortune and joy. Pay attention during the Chinese New Year as you will see red everywhere in celebration.

Red is also adored in India, specifically in Indian weddings. They tie the color to love and believe it to ignite a 'divine spark'. Brides normally wear red along with a red vermilion on the forehead which symbolizes marriage, fertility, prosperity and marital bliss.

In most African cultures, red symbolizes death and grief. In Nigeria and South Africa, red means violence and sacrifice. The flag of South Africa has red in it as a reminder of the violence that occurred during its fight for freedom. The Pan-African flag contains red for a similar reason, but also to symbolize the noble blood that unites the African people.

Russia uses tons and tons of red. The word red, krasni, was used to describe something beautiful, good or honorable. Red Square is the most important square in Moscow. Most Orthodox homes also have a "red corner", or a krasni ugol where they keep their religious materials. The country has an entirely red flag and even dye their eggs red for Easter every year.

Love. Duty. Success. Prosperity. Strength. Our current world cultures and religions prove that red is definitely a primary color when it comes to human communication.

BEHAVIOR

How do we physically behave when we're in a red environment? What does the body actually do?

A study was done by the University of Rochester in 2008 proving the color red actually enhanced attraction.

"Under all of the conditions, the women shown framed by or wearing red were rated significantly more attractive and sexually desirable by men than the exact same women shown with other colors. When wearing red, the woman was also more likely to score an invitation to the prom and to be treated to a more expensive outing." -Andrew J. Elliot

People have one primary response to the color red: attention.

Physiologically, we flush red in the face when we're angry, nervous or even 'blushing' when we find someone attractive or are embarrassed.

We stop at stop signs. We stop for firetrucks. We read notices.

In most cases, we are very responsive physically when we are triggered by red. You see a pretty redhead at the bar, or you see a stop sign, or you see a red striped snake...these types of stimuli will cause you to act quickly in one way or another.

Andrew J. Elliot at the University of Rochester proved our reactions to red in a negative way when it comes to test taking. If students saw any kind of red before a test, they tested poorly.

Now we understand that the color red can raise our blood pressure and heart rate, prompt our immediate attention and make us physically react. Our behavior when seeing red is one of action.

NATURE

In nature, we see reds mostly in birds, fruits, primates, flowers and leaves in the fall.

As summer fades, the levels of phosphates in the plant decreases, bringing life back into the stem and trunk of a plant and out of its leaves. Since the sap/sugar production changes, light pigments are reflected differently, resulting in a changing of the color. These pigments are called anthocyanins.

Now, you can see your tree change and thank the incredible process of your tree going into hibernation for its gorgeous autumn display!

These same pigments are in red grapes that, when fermented, create red wine. (The grapes of this category containing anthocyanins in their flesh are named teinturiers, if you'd like to impress at your next wine tasting.)

Most animals can see red, but some have what's called dichromacy, meaning they see blues and yellows - not reds. Some research even suggests that the red cape of a bullfighter is just seen as a muted object by a bull. It can't see red!

We also tend to associate red with ripened fruit. This possibly explains why certain animal species have developed trichromacy, to be able to see red to detect fruit that's ready to eat.

Red is seen in nature as the most widespread signaling color of attention in the natural world. It's easily visible against blue (like the sky) and green (like foliage).

HEALING

Is the color red used in healing?

You've probably heard of infrared light being used in a lot of cases of healing and pain reduction. Since red is so close to infrared, this is a great healing modality to research. I personally use an infrared light pad to bring down pain levels and soothe soreness.

An infrared sauna can also be a great way to detoxify the

body. This type of sauna uses light to make heat, warming your body directly instead of just the air around you. Research shows that this process more closely mimics a fever within the body, so it's a different type of sweat than a normal sauna. I use a Sunlighten infrared sauna because of its use of low, mid and high infrared light and low EMF output.

Avicenna was one of the earliest fathers of modern medicine, author of The Canon of Medicine (1025) and The Book Of Healing (1027). He believed color was vital to both diagnosis of disease and its treatment. He developed a chart that related color temperature to the physicality of the body. Red, he stated, moved the blood. This led to his observation that someone with a nosebleed or heavy bleeding should not look at reds as it would increase blood flow.

Edwin Babbitt, pioneer in chromotherapy (color/light therapy), created a much more prescriptive concordance of light use in healing. Red was found to be a stimulant, most notably with blood but with some affect on nerves. He used red to treat paralysis, physical exhaustion and chronic rheumatism.

There's a fascinating technique introduced by Charles Klotsche called the 49th Vibrational Technique, or to put it simply, 'Color Medicine'. The theory is that by finding the vibrational frequency of a specific color, it can help a specific part of the body regenerate or balance.

That's why I'm putting in the musical note equivalent of all the light spectrum colors in these chapters so you can do your own experiments!

Red, according to Klotsche, can activate all five senses as well as the increased production of red blood cells. He also uses red to counteract x-ray and ultraviolet burns. The color red, according to his research, vibrates at 436 trillion times per second.

"The visible light spectrum with its beneficial frequencies for the human body provides the preventing tool for healing. Color Medicine is truly, the medicine of the future." - Klotsche C., *Color Medicine.*

A new therapy called PDT (photodynamic therapy), developed by Thomas Dougherty, Ph.D, has recently come to the forefront. Certain photosensitive chemicals injected intravenously accumulate within cancer cells and identify these cells when exposed to ultraviolet light. These cells then exclusively destroy the cancer cells they are in when activated by red light. Since red light wavelengths are longer, it penetrates tissue more deeply than any other color. His technique is now used all around the world.

MUSIC

The color red correlates to the musical note "G". We also tend to resonate with slower frequencies, or lower sounds, in the audible range of red. The "G" of nature can be heard from crickets.

A friend of mine actually created songs using each visible light spectrum color and I was blown away by my physical reaction to red!

FILM

In film, red is called "The Caffeinated Color". Since it lies on the longest end of the visible light spectrum, it feels like it's coming at us.

The color does not have a moral imperative, it fuels anyone wearing it or in its environment, like the red shoes worn by both Dorothy and the witch in *The Wizard Of Oz*.

Red can empower the good guy or the bad guy.

When I think of red, I see the red apple from *Snow White and the Seven Dwarfs*, Jessica Rabbit or the little girl in the red coat in *Schindler's List*.

The warmer the red in film, the more it's seen as sensuous and full of passion. Think *Shakespeare In Love* with the warm red bedspread. The colder the red, the more murderous it will feel.

More recently, a television show called *Only Murders In The Building* has been a favorite to watch because of its focus on color psychology. They use blue, green, yellow and red. The three main characters are each exclusively tied to blue, green or yellow. So where does red come in? Red is actually the character of murder, present in almost every scene. It's a very unique way to use the color in the show by making it a main character that's never "seen".

When a filmmaker knows what they're doing, they will use red to prompt action, passion, empowerment and even murder.

WHY YOU LOVE IT

You may absolutely love the color red and it could be for a variety of reasons!

The positive traits associated with red are strength,

passion, courage, survival, energy, excitement, masculinity and warmth. This color may give you the feeling of power, attractiveness or even help you to take action.

You are a very driven person who likes to live life in the fast lane. Easy to react, take action and sometimes even steamroll, you are a go-getter who takes charge.

Your life has probably become much more active with the color around you, and you could possible love it because you came from a color-rich culture that uses red. Or maybe you grew up in a very gray home, gray school and moved into a gray office building that made you seek out more color, like red, so you'd actually feel something.

No matter the reason, a love for the color red can be incredibly helpful in integrating us into the present of our reality.

WHY YOU HATE IT

A lot of people shrink back and turn away from red. It's seen as "too much", too violent or even too passionate.

The negative traits can be anger ("seeing red"), annoyance, exhaustion, arguments, aggression, confrontation, defiance, overwhelm and stress.

If you grew up in an argumentative home, I think there'd definitely be a natural aversion to this color.

Or, if you work in a profession with a lot of red - like a police officer, fireman or even a crime scene investigator - it's probably the last color you want around you.

Even if you hate it, understanding why will give you options. For example, you may not want it in your home, but maybe you choose watermelon for your child's sport snack to pep him up for physical activity.

IMPLEMENTING IT INTO YOUR LIFE

Color is a strategic tool we can implement thoughtfully into our daily lives.

In the case of red, after all we've been through with its many variations, you can see both positive and negative. This is true for every color, by the way.

For example, when talking with someone who is really concerned with a family member's behavior - fights, frustration, anger - the first thing I do is ask what colors are in the home.

Can you imagine trying to relax and sleep at night in a red bedroom? Would red help or hurt a marriage in conflict?

Maybe red wouldn't be the best color for a bedroom wall, but it may be the perfect color to wear at your next meeting to keep people's attention. See what I mean?

Red will induce people into a fight or flight reaction. So keep that in mind when putting red into your environment.

Be thoughtful and monitor your own reactions.

Throughout the day, is there a specific hour or two where you feel on the verge of a very insistent nap? What if you changed your desktop to a red photo?

Small changes like this can drastically impact our behavior in a very positive way.

As you can see, there are mountains to unpack with the color red. It's a very dominant color used in our world today as it always has been - in large quantities.

What I love the most about the color is that it can

strengthen any goal, desire or truth. It empowers anything. If someone is too much in their head or has a hard time acting on a goal, this is the color I pull out for them to start using.

If I'm on stage and need someone to pay attention, I wear red. This is why the *TEDx* stage is red! It makes us center in the moment and see what's really happening.

The undeniable physical, behavioral, scientific and emotional reactions we have to red prove it to be a key color in our communication.

Will you start using red as a part of your language? And what aspects of your life are you being spoken to with this color that you haven't noticed before?

ORANGE
THE COLOR OF BALANCE & THE EXOTIC

Of all the colors in the world, orange was the one I liked the least. My clients usually echoed the sentiment.

"No! Not orange! Anything but orange!". I totally get it.

Orange is not an easy color to love for most people, at least when they think of putting it on their skin.

When I finally started teaching color, I honestly dreaded having to add orange into my closet. But of course, the more I made myself study the color, the more I grew to appreciate it.

If you had to associate one word with orange, I'd say it would overwhelmingly be "balance".

Which made me wonder why it repelled me so much in the beginning - and why it does for many others when they think about wearing it. Are we repulsed because of our own lack of life balance? Probably.

Orange is a color that brings life, comfort and a welcoming feeling into any space. While I may not paint a wall orange, adding a vase filled with orange flowers would potentially be the perfect touch to evoke the feeling desired.

The color usually indicates that someone is very

thoughtful and considerate of others. We also tend to perceive someone wearing orange as strong in their health and vitality.

I find orange to be a wonderful change of color in a wardrobe. People respond to it immediately. Whether it's a spouse, friend or local event gathering, you will see much more natural interaction when wearing orange.

SCIENCE

In the visible light spectrum, orange lies between red and yellow - two psychological primaries. Since red represents the physical and yellow the emotions, our grounded reaction to orange is somewhat bizarre, isn't it?

Orange is called a *tertiary* color since you have to mix two primaries to see it. It lies between the wavelengths of 585 and 620 nanometers. The compliment to the color orange in terms of pigment is azure, a greenish blue.

Two researchers from the Max Planck Institute for Psycholinguistics wanted to prove that associations with certain objects influence our ability to see a color. They worked with orange and yellow.

Half of the participants saw photos of items like carrots with their true orange hue.

The other half saw the same photographs of items in more of a yellow tone.

The yellow participants still called the color they saw, which was yellow, 'orange'.

This experiment proved that objects we specifically associate with a color do indeed influence our perception of it. Probably because we process visual information through the brain centers that categorize information, creating identification.

Now let's talk about chickens. This amazing girl Lena wanted to examine the evolution of color vision in vertebrates for a middle school assignment. She knew the technical science of how many colors vertebrates, like chickens, could see: red, green, blue and ultraviolet.

This has been discovered by putting different animals' eyes under a microscope, seeing how many rods and codes they have, and therefore approximating how many colors they can see. That didn't take into account, however, the actual physical function of the visual system when the brain is involved.

So she went to her chickens and sheep. A bird and a mammal who supposedly have very different color perceptions. For reference, sheep have two cone cells (*dichromat*), humans have three (*trichromat*) and chickens have four (*tetrochromat*). Yes, a chicken sees better than you.

Test one was the animals differentiating between black and white. The results were that 80% of the time these animals were able to tell them apart easily.

Test two was between green and purple. Again, both animals scored over 80%.

Test three was between orange and red. This should have been pretty much impossible for sheep, but they still had about a 50% success rate. And the chickens could tell them apart with 85.8% success.

For the most part, there are very few experiments conducted with the color orange. There's not much research to find. My hope is that this book will get into the hands of students all over the world who will start experimenting and researching orange and will report back their findings!

I would love to see someone's response going from a red room, to a blue room, to an orange room to see what happened to their heart rate, blood pressure and mood. From my personal research, I would bet money that if each room had a kitchen with stools, the orange room would be the one where the person would sit the fastest.

Maybe we'll be able to update this book with proof soon!

HISTORY

Orange began its journey with the Ancient Egyptians. They used an orange mineral pigment called *realgar* for their tomb paintings. Much later, this same pigment was found in manuscript coloring done by medieval artists.

Another orange pigment used in ancient times was *orpiment*, a golden-yellow hued mineral. Many alchemists believed that it held the secret to creating gold. *Orpiment* was traded throughout the Roman Empire. It was also used as a medicine in some countries before it was discovered to have such high arsenic content.

Oranges became associated with the color in the sixteenth century, when Portuguese merchants brought orange trees to Europe. The first written record was in 1502 for clothing purchased by Margaret Tudor. Before that, it was called *saffron* or *yellow-red*.

The color was made famous by The House of Orange-Nassau, one of the most influential families in the 16th and 17th centuries. They were named after the Principality of Orange, a small state in southern France founded in 1163. The town associated strongly with the color because it was on the 'orange route' where the fruit was shipped from southern ports like Marseille.

Artists used *orpiment* for their orange color tones until the

19th century when other sources became available. Painters moved away from it quickly because it did not work well with *verdigris* or *azurite,* common pigments used and mixed to create other colors.

French scientist Louis Vauquelin discovered *crocoite,* another mineral, that aided in the creation of the synthetic pigment *chrome orange* in 1797. Other pigments were later invented using *cadmium sulphide* combined with *cadmium selenite*; creating *cobalt red, cobalt yellow* and *cobalt orange.* What's so important about this is that it offered artists the ability to do something outstanding for the first time: paint outdoors.

Many impressionist and post-impressionists painters favored orange for its exoticism, the most recognizable being Vincent van Gogh. He loved using orange to capture the sunlight of Provence, and he made quite the statement painting an orange moon and stars in a cobalt sky.

"There is no blue without yellow and without orange."
-Vincent van Gogh.

The most stunning artistic creation of the color orange I've seen is *Flaming June,* created by Lord Frederic Leighton during the Victorian Era. Other beautiful works are *Pamona* by Nicolas Fouché and *Impression Sunrise* by Claude Monet. The Pre-Raphaelite movement of artists in England, 1848, held Elizabeth Siddal as the symbol of their movement because of her flowing orange-red hair.

Orange was the color for the *Stradivarius* violin. To this day, no one knows the ingredients Anthony Stradivari used to create it. If you are unfamiliar, he was an Italian instrument maker in the 18th century whose violins now sell for 2-3 million dollars. Some believe this unique orange varnish is what gives the instruments their unique, exquisite sound.

More recently, Mark Rothko's *Orange, Red, Yellow* painting sold for 86.9 million dollars!

BEHAVIOR

I don't think I've ever heard someone say orange is their favorite color.

Look around at the supermarket, school, even your home and orange probably won't be a standout color you see.

But what if you knew this color could supercharge your brain?

There's a light-sensitive cell or photopigment in our eyes called *melanopsin*. *Melanopsin* is a neuro-hormone that signals the pineal to suppress melatonin production when activated by short wavelengths components of light (like sunrise). This helps us regulate our sleeping and waking behaviors based on light, which is why we wake up with the sun.

So, in 2014, researchers from the University of Liège, Belgium, and INSERM Stem Cell and Brain Research Institute, France, decided to test how *melanopsin* affected our brains.

They observed 16 people for a week while regulating their sleeping and waking patterns. After 8 hours of sleep, they were exposed to white light for 5 minutes to reset their light history. They were put under green light (515 nm) while performing auditory and memory tasks under an fMRI scan. Before each recording, they were exposed to 10-minute blasts of either blue (461 nm) or orange (589 nm) light. The subjects under orange light showed greater brain activity in several regions of the frontal lobes that register alertness and cognition. Blue light caused the reverse effect.

"Ultimately, these findings argue for the use and design of lighting systems to optimize cognitive performance." -INSERM

Can you imagine how much better our test-taking would have been if we would have known to wear orange? Or even using citrus essential oils on our skin...since they've shown positive effects on alertness?

Studies like this are pretty conclusive proof that color affects behavior. And I believe it's information like this that will make us the ones leading the revolution of color language for years to come.

By taking 'ammunition' like this into schools, universities, libraries and local governments, we could quite possibly introduce this new language as a commonality to everyone's benefit.

I've been shouting orange from the rooftops for years as I think it's the most underrated color. Hopefully, that will soon change.

CURRENT CULTURE & RELIGION

Most people in the United States associate Halloween with orange because it represents pumpkins and most decorations of the holiday. It's seen in America and Europe as the color of amusement - tied to fairs, theaters and even clowns.

Orange is the national color of the Netherlands. On royal birthdays, the flag of red, white and blue is flown with an orange pennant above it. On the day of April 27th, Amsterdam becomes a sea of orange. They proclaim, "Oranje boven, oranje boven. Leve the Koning!" (Orange on top, orange on top. Long live the king!)

When it comes to Native American culture, orange is the color of family and considered energetic, cheerful, joyful and anti-depressive.

The dye most associated with this color in Asia is *saffron*, which is the most expensive dye available.

India views this as the sacred color of Hindus. Yogis, gurus and godly men wear saffron robes paired with saffron turbans. It is seen as the color of fire - burning out all impurities - and the quest for light. It is the dominant color in the Indian flag, symbolizing courage and renunciation.

Many Hindu and Buddhist monks and holy men across Asia wear this color. In Buddhism, orange is the color of transformation, even worn by Buddha himself and his followers in the 5th century. The color, according to Buddhist scriptures, must be sourced only from roots/tubers, plants, bark, leaves, flowers or fruits.

What's so fascinating is the tone of orange worn.

The monks of Tibet wear the most colorful saffron and red robes. The monks of Japan wear lighter yellow or saffron. The monks of Southeast Asia wear *ochre* or *saffron*. And the monks of Thailand wear brownish *ochre*.

In China, this is the color of transformation tied to Confucianism. It is the blend of yellow and red, light and fire, spirituality and sensuality.

All crew members of the International Space Station wear orange.

NATURE

We most often equate orange with food in nature.

The group of molecules that create the orange color in food are called *carotenes*, from a photosynthetic pigment. (Think of oranges, squash, carrots, cantaloupe, sweet potatoes and tangerines.)

Carotene is absorbed by the small intestine and turned into retinal. This is probably why you've heard that carrots improve eye-sight.

Did you know that the orange is a man made fruit? It's a hybrid of a *pomelo* and a *mandarin*! Just as weird is that carrots were originally purple or white. The Dutch introduced the orange variety in 1721.

There are many beautiful tones of orange in nature's flowers, leaves and even animals. Think of the the *poppy* flower or the *Bengal* tiger.

We mainly associate orange with the sense of taste. Seasonings of *curry*, *paprika*, *saffron* and *turmeric* make us almost taste this color.

HEALING

Now that you've gotten a great introduction to the body's physical response to color, I'm going to present you with some pretty stunning research I've found in regards to color being involved in healing practices.

A very fascinating therapist who uses colors, Noah Goldhirsh, has experimented with color therapy for years. She has found orange to help people struggling with a lack of energy and to help bring balance back to the body.

It is a driving and stimulating color, so it's not a dominant color to use when working with children with hyperactivity or attention deficit disorder, she states. She's even found wearing orange can help women with cramping and an orange bra can help with breastfeeding!

Robert Gerard, Ph.D., wanted to prove that color creates reactions in the body. He used techniques like the electroencephalogram and beaming light onto the skin to test what would happen. Warm colors, like orange, helped lift the moods of those with neurasthenia and reactive depression. People exposed to warm light colors increased muscle tone, blood pressure, respiratory movements, cortical activation and woke up their autonomic nervous system.

Klotsche states that orange helps release trapped energy in organs. The color raises the pulse rate, but not the blood pressure. It can also be used for emotional uplifting. He has found orange to vibrate at 473 trillion times per second.

MUSIC

The color orange correlates to the musical note "A". We can easily hear this from listening to the harp.

FILM

We tend to associate orange with more exotic locations onscreen, so it's an easy filter to put on a movie to help us feel that way instantly. In film, orange is called "The Sweet and Sour Color".

It supports a very warm and welcoming congenial atmosphere. You can see this in the movie *The Best Exotic Marigold Hotel*. It can, however, also make us feel trapped and toxic, like the sky in *Blade Runner*.

In recent television, we saw plenty of orange in the show *Orange Is The New Black*. Solidifying our association of orange as a prison color, this show tried to adjust our perceptions of inmates. It highlighted the bond between them, how they worked as a team and made the cell block feel like home.

There are very few tests where orange elicited a negative response with the film students of Patti Bellantoni, funnily enough. Only when it got to shades of traffic cone orange. It's a color we don't have many feelings about - we are generally okay with it.

It brings a feeling of sensuality and the exotic, but not in the lustful or sexual way red does. Orange makes us feel very relaxed and welcomed. Like we're at home or on a desirable vacation. This is why marigolds planted in front of a home tend to make it sell faster!

"As light, however, orange has a double-edged quality. How we feel at sunset is not just a romanticized cliche. Something actually happens to us physically when we watch the intense brightness of the near-white sun transform itself into a glowing rich orange in the sky. Glowing orange light (and its associations with the sun) can take us on a visceral ride that warms and expands our emotional field." -Patti Bellantoni, *If It's Purple, Someone's Gunna Die*

Isn't that interesting? Orange in our environment not only gives us a physical reaction but an emotional one.

How many times does someone say a romantic date would

be walking on the beach at sunset? Or when we retire, don't we think of a sunset over water somewhere? I definitely do.

WHY YOU LOVE IT

If you're someone who loves orange, chances are you grew up with it around you - either in your culture or where you lived. You're probably attracted to sandy beaches and sunsets or keep it as art in your office as an escape.

The positive traits associated with orange are warmth, friendliness, energy, fun, playfulness, mischievousness, sociability and abundance.

This color may make you feel comfortable, homey, and the house everyone loves to come to because it feels like family.

No matter the reason, a love for the color orange can be very beneficial to keeping your life balanced and warm.

WHY YOU HATE IT

Prison uniforms and traffic cones. Sometimes, that's why we can't stand orange.

The negative traits associated with this color can be childishness, frivolity, unrefined or cheap.

You may hate clowns. Or fairs and circus'. Because people use orange in these types of entertainment, it can put a bad taste in our mouths.

Even if you detest it, studying the color has hopefully helped you appreciate the strengths of it and how it can sometimes exemplify the opposite of your experiences.

Maybe you can change its definition in your life in the future, especially in your home environment.

IMPLEMENTING IT INTO YOUR LIFE

Orange is the quiet hero of the color world. It says heart and home with a flair, and this is how I encourage you to use it.

Whether it's dahlia's on your kitchen table, or an orange couch for movie nights, this is a color that's great in the home.

If you're teaching a class that's full of gray and blue, think about adding orange touches throughout your classroom. Have everyone bring in an orange and teach a lesson on it.

We don't have to keep orange (or gray for that matter) in prison. Forcing the color to be something that, in its organic nature, it truly isn't.

Orange can bring ease. It can invite people in.

So feel free to wear it to give you more energy. To make spaces feel like home. And to even motivate you for that next vacation!

As you can see, orange is a color that is very misunderstood for the most part. It can help someone feel at ease, welcomed and full of balanced energy. This makes it a key color in color language.

If I'm working with someone who wants their clients to feel more balanced, guess which color I recommend? You guessed it.

How much more powerful can a color get? The next time you plant flowers in your garden or head out to a family reunion, think about how orange can support your intentions.

What do you think? Is orange maybe your new secret weapon? Will you experiment with using this in your home to see how your family responds?

YELLOW
THE COLOR OF JOY & CAUTION

FUNNILY ENOUGH, this was the last color chapter I wrote. I avoided it until the end!

Not because I don't like yellow, but because it is a psychological primary that affects the emotions and nervous system. Is it any surprise that with a looming book deadline and pressing brand launch that I wrote this last?

Yellow is one of the most surprising colors because it has so much flexibility in its meaning. It can mean confidence, positivity and optimism...but also caution, anxiety and nervousness.

Since it effects our emotions and has an impact on the nervous system - making it the strongest psychological primary color and a key color in communication.

SCIENCE

Yellow lies between orange and green in the visible light spectrum, resonating between 575-590 nanometers. Yellow's complimentary color is violet or blue, depending on the system used.

When we see yellow, it's because the green and red cones in the retina of the eye are near their peak sensitivity. They call this "excitement". Besides white, this is the only other color that is the very top excitement the eye can experience.

The RGB color model, used to create color on television and computer screens, shows that yellow is created by combining red and green. Yellow is also a colorblind-safe color.

Interestingly, printers only use four colors to create every color: cyan, magenta, yellow and black (CMYK). But the printing process of yellow is completely different then how it's created on screens. This ink is called *process yellow* and cannot be replicated by the RGB color model.

As we will read in the blue chapter, certain LED frequencies based on blue light can cause significant eye strain. In the 1960's, Pickett Brand developed something called *Eye Saver Yellow*, which was a slide rule that produced Angstrom 5600. This was a specific yellow color that reflects blue wavelengths and promotes optimum eye-ease. I think this is a pretty solid claim that yellow is the perfect balance color to blue.

Did you know that yellow is officially the color reserved for stars? F. G. W. Struve classified stars as *flavae*, or yellow, who had a modern spectral range from F5 to K0 in 1827. Later, the Strömgren photometric system for stellar classification put a 'y' classification, or filter, that centers at a wavelength of 550 nanometers. Stars are officially yellow!

HISTORY

Yellow made its start with humans back in prehistoric art. Cave drawings painted with yellow *ochre* from clay to be exact.

One of the first art pieces was of a yellow horse in the Lascaux Cave in France thought to be over 17,000 years old.

Ancient Egypt used yellow extensively because of its resemblance to gold, which they believed to be eternal and imperishable. People believed the bones of the gods were made of gold. Egyptians used lots of yellow in their tomb paintings and it was mainly found in the painting of female faces. The males were colored brown. This pattern of facial painting is also seen with ancient Roman art and the murals of Pompeii.

A small paintbox with *orpiment*, orange-yellow arsenic sulfide, was found in the tomb of King Tutankhamun.

Strangely, yellow became well-known as the color tied to Judas Iscariot, the disciple who betrayed Christ, even though his clothing color is never mentioned in the Bible. That started to culturally tie yellow to feelings of envy, jealousy and duplicity.

It came as no surprise that the Renaissance period was a time of marking non-Christians, such as Jews, with the color yellow. This is why Jews were marked with yellow stars in Nazi Germany.

In Spain during the 16th century, people accused of heresy or false claims were forced to come before the Spanish Inquisition dressed in a yellow cape.

The 18th and 19th centuries started shifting the meaning of yellow for the better. Traditional materials to make the color, which included cow urine, *arsenic* and *saffron*, started being replaced with synthetics. Examples are *Naples yellow* and *chrome yellow* in 1809 and *cadmium yellow* in 1820.

Paintings such as *A Young Girl Reading*, *Rain, Steam and Speed - The Great Western Railway* and *Sunflowers* brought completely new dimensions to how color was viewed by the world.

We have our term "yellow" from the Proto-Germanic word *gelwaz* that became *geolu* in Old English.

Vincent Van Gogh was, funnily enough, an avid studier of color theory. And he believed that any two colors that formed achromatic white were perfectly complementary to each other.

With this theory in mind, yellow's perfect complimentary would be violet (RYB).

If we go specifically into a balance of light, however, the complement to yellow would be blue (RGB).

Painters will usually say yellow's complement, therefore, is indigo or blue-violet.

Van Gogh, a particular fan of yellow, stated that, "Now we are having beautiful warm, windless weather that is very beneficial to me. The sun, a light that for lack of a better word I can only call yellow, bright sulfur yellow, pale lemon gold. How beautiful yellow is!"

In 1895, a new type of art came on the scene - colored comics. It started in New York newspapers who debuted color printing. One of the first comics, *Mikey Dugan* became known as the "yellow kid" because of the nightdress he wore.

This evolved into *yellow journalism*, a type of journalism rarely based on facts, but more-so focused on attention-grabbing, exaggerated, outlandish claims.

Yellow became much more desirable in the 20th century because it is a color with extremely high visibility. It can be seen from far distances and at high speeds. It became a very common color for cars and even emergency vehicles.

Here's what's really weird. We talked about most yellow paint sources before synthetics being toxic, right? *Naples Yellow, Cadmium Yellow, Chrome Yellow, King's Yellow*...all of which became known to be very toxic and even fatal to use.

I would think creating yellow dye for food coloring would then obviously be sourced from something safe, like *saffron* or *turmeric*, right?

Instead, we use *Tartrazine*. We use it to color potato chips, corn, cereal, candies, popcorn, mustard, soft drinks, soap and even medicine. It's labeled as "color", "tartrazine" or "E102". Look for it, because at least in the US it has to be labeled due to so many reports of health problems. And don't be fooled by "E110", Europe. This yellow food coloring is sourced from aromatic hydrocarbons from petroleum.

BEHAVIOR

In a survey taken in the year 2000, people largely did not identify yellow as their favorite color. Only 6% did. We can see historically why that may be. I tend to have a brain freeze thinking about the possibility of color associations being passed down in our genes. Otherwise, why would we have such native instincts to things like this?

When we focus our attention on yellow, positive behavior changes can happen. We can feel uplifted, optimistic and even feel a boost to our self-esteem. On the negative side, however, if we are in a bad space or prone to irritation, it can cause us to feel irritable, depressed or even obsessive.

According to memory studies, we tend to more easily remember red and yellow-colored objects - especially long term. Warm colors are more stimulating to us as they are used more as attention-getters in society and stimulate the sympathetic nervous system, as opposed to cooler colors. This could possibly be due to *aposematism*, which is the coloring of animals as warning signs. We equate these two colors with most dangerous species like snakes, frogs and insects.

There was a very interesting experiment done at a college campus. Two researchers wanted to prove that color would positively affect the students. Since most buildings and interior spaces at a university are white, gray or brown, this was an opportunity to bring color psychology into the environment to see if it really made a difference.

One room, in particular, was painted yellow. It was called "Point Break".

The 490 students polled stated a few interesting things after the experiment:

- 332 said the color in the room made them restless or too excited
- 305 said the room was their favorite spot on campus
- 375 said the communication between them and their friends actually strengthened in that room

From what we know about yellow, it's pretty easy to accept that for some people, the wall color would be overstimulating. The color pushed them emotionally and their nervous system responded negatively. This could especially be the case with hyperactivity.

Let's also look at the positives this color created: favoritism and communication. Feeling happy in the space - therefore the room being their favorite. Communicating well in the space - therefore the strengthening of friendships.

Clearly, yellow is a dominant color in color communication.

I forgot to tell you that the next highest vote for a room that strengthened friendships was at 48 votes. That means

Point Break got 7.8 times more votes than its closest competition!

Yellow had a huge impact on these college students in a positive way.

CURRENT CULTURE & RELIGION

In China, yellow is seen as the most esteemed color. It is one of their sacred colors, denoting happiness, glory and wisdom. They believe in the five directions of the compass and yellow signifies the middle, vital to the center. China is called "The Middle Kingdom". The palace of the Emperor was thought to be in the exact center of the world.

According to legend, the first Emperor of China was called *The Yellow Emperor*. This led to Puyi, the last emperor of China (1967) sharing his memories as a child being surrounded by yellow.

> "It made me understand from my most tender age that I was of a unique essence, and it instilled in me the consciousness of my 'celestial nature' which made me different from every other human." -Puyi

After the Song dynasty, bright yellow is only worn by the Emperor. And, unlike Hollywood, the White House or even Buckingham palace, distinguished guests here are honored with a yellow carpet.

Currently in Chinese pop culture the term *yellow movie*, strangely refers to pornographic films. Don't ask me why - I'm not going to research that.

As a blond-haired person myself, I can tell you that yellow

hair was used throughout Greece and Rome as a symbol of the sun. Men and women in ancient Greece would actually dye their hair yellow to appear more like the sun gods Helios and Apollo whom they worshiped. In ancient Rome, however, prostitutes were required to bleach their hair so they could be easily identified.

When it became fashionable for aristocratic women to bleach their hair, it's pretty clear why the word was quickly changed from yellow to "blond", "light", "fair" or even "golden". (Now I'm wondering if the meaning of *yellow movie* in China is pretty darn clear.)

I find it bizarre that us blond folk are widely seen as naive or less intelligent since yellow is a color that actually boosts the intellect, increases concentration and inspires creativity.

No matter the culture, history or location, we as human beings most easily associate yellow with sunlight. Warmth, joy, optimism...we're drawn to the natural hue of yellow as the light that should surround us during the day.

In English, words like "brilliant" and "bright" mean that someone is intelligent. In Islam, yellow symbolizes wisdom. European universities very commonly put their science faculty in yellow gowns and caps to symbolize reason.

Since I've found yellow to help people see themselves in the future, to regain hope and to brighten the mind, I can easily agree with these definitions.

NATURE

We talked a bit about *carotenoids* in the red chapter and that is the case in nature with the color yellow as well. These yellow pigments are specifically called *xanthophylls*. They are yellow, orange and red pigments created by plants, algae, bacteria and fungi.

Yellow, orange, and red leaves in autumn display their *carotenoid* pigments more and more as the chlorophyll drains from the leaves in winter with the increasing cold. The same process takes place with bananas and lemons as they ripen.

Cartenoid pigments give flowers like St. John's Wort, daffodils, buttercups, canary eggs and egg yolks their yellow coloring.

Most animals that display yellow colors in their hair, feathers or egg yolks are due to the food they eat, which contain *xanthophylls*. Chicken farmers even supplement their feed with lutein (which has high amounts of *xanthophylls*) to make the egg yolks more strikingly yellow!

A few species of fish have yellow coloring: yellowtail, yellowfin tuna, smallmouth yellowfish, gold angelfish, gold arowana, gold barb, yellow tang, lemonpeel angelfish and the yellow watchman goby. There's also a surprising amount of yellow in ocean coral and starfish.

Yellow in these natural elements makes us quite happy and feels like sunshine.

There is a type of yellow, however, specifically combined with black, that instinctively makes us want to run. Bees, yellow-jackets, yellow-fever mosquito and snakes.

Maybe it's been passed down in our DNA for survival. But one thing we know for sure, yellow and black are huge warning indicators.

In yellow clothing throughout history, dyes were very commonly sourced from *turmeric* and *saffron*. *Turmeric* was used for monks' robes, and is now used as a food coloring for mustard as well as a curry spice which gives it its signature yellow tones.

Saffron, made from the dried red stigma of the *Crocus*

sativus flower, is very hard to turn into dye. 150 flowers create one single gram. Its use was described in a botanical reference during the rule of King Ashurbanipal of the Neo-Assyrian Empire in 669 BC. It was also used during the time of Buddha. After his death, his followers decreed that monks should wear robes colored with *saffron*. The tradition began of senior Buddhist monks' robes being dyed with *saffron*, while ordinary monks' robes were dyed with *turmeric*.

I have not been able to find such a variety of dye sources in nature of any other color. The most, unmistakably, are yellow.

From the *Reseda luteola* (dyer's weed), the *Garcinia* tree, the *Quercitron* tree, *Turmeric* and *Saffron*, these are just a few that help produce yellow colored dye.

The actual pigment comes from the red variety of *carotenoids* inside the plant. Specifically with saffron, the dye shades range from red to orange to yellow, depending on the type of saffron and the process used. Very similar to *Tyrian purple* in a way.

It's grown all over the world, from the Mediterranean to Iran, to India, northern Europe and even the United States - usually grown by the Pennsylvania Dutch.

HEALING

Many healing practices strategically use the color yellow. This includes alternative therapies for supporting the chakras, stone healing work and color therapy. I've heard many healers reference yellow as relating to both the digestive system and solar plexus.

Many cultures practiced light therapy - Egypt, Greece, China and India. Charaka, the ancient Ayurvedic physician

(6th century BC), used sunlight to treat a variety of diseases. The Greeks used both direct and indirect exposure to sunlight for healing through sunlight and colored stones, dyes and ointments. Avicenna later found that yellow reduced muscular pain and inflammation.

Edwin Babbitt used yellow chromotherapy as a purging treatment for bronchial struggles, a laxative and an emetic.

A study by the National Library of Medicine stated that dawn-simulating light (DsL) had the most positive effects on waking someone up, improving cognitive morning function as well as mood and overall well-being (unlike LED or dim light). This research encouraged me to get a DsL light for my desk. I keep it on while I'm working so my body can have the positive effects to the exposure. It's also shown to help with Seasonal Affective Disorder.

Returning to Klotsche and the 49th Vibrational Technique, he describes yellow as a stimulant for the sensory and motor nervous system. Pretty easy to accept since we've proven the notion throughout this chapter. He uses yellow light on the body to tone the muscles, activate the lymph glands and improve the digestive system. Klotsche has found yellow to vibrate at 547 trillion times per second.

MUSIC

The color yellow correlates to the musical note "A#". This can be found in wooden flutes or Reggae music.

FILM

In film, yellow is known as "The Contrary Color" because, as we've learned, it can mean two very different things.

It can symbolize exuberance and joy like we've talked about, but also obsession. As we've seen throughout history, the color can cause polar opposite reactions unlike any other color in the visible light spectrum. It is the color of sunshine as well as caution signs.

"Yellow is the color longest remembered and most despised." - Dr. Harry Hepner, Professor of Psychology of Advertising at Syracuse University

To find a usable yellow tone, the key is desaturation. The less intense color you choose, the better. Too much green in a yellow color used onscreen will feel repulsive. Too much neon and it will feel very cautionary.

Yellow is a shade where the lighter you go, the more elegant it will come across.

We see the exuberant joy of yellow in Billy Elliot. Or the bright yellow brick road on the way to Emerald City in *The Wizard Of Oz* - signaling both happiness and trials on their path ahead. There is even strong tones of agitation and caution in *Kill Bill* all around Uma Thurman's character.

In the second season of *The Flight Attendant*, the main character Cassie is in yellow many times throughout the show - especially when she goes to her mind space. Certain scenes are completely saturated with the color. This is due to her double-sided nature, where she wants to live harmoniously, but where she also wants to destroy herself.

WHY YOU LOVE IT

If you love the color yellow, I think I can accurately assume that you're a very joyful, happy person. You are probably very social, interactive and carry energy throughout your day. The other possibility is that you may have come from a painful or traumatic past, turning to the positive and creating a joyful atmosphere for your family and friends.

Yellow-lovers are sunny people. They're usually hard to upset and will always look at the bright side of things. If anything, their biggest challenge is slowing down and taking things seriously. They usually attract partners who are more grounded and serious to balance them out.

You now know yellow is one of your greatest friends for a reason - something you can carry forward with you to support your focus and future.

WHY YOU HATE IT

If you hate yellow, I'm sure you hate bees too. That's usually how it works out!

It may be from a bad experience, or you may not like how you feel around the color. Hopefully, this chapter has shown you the positive things yellow can do for your life and body.

But don't jump in too quickly! If you deal with hyperactivity, depression or ADD/ADHD, use with caution. Do something a bit more balancing, like bringing orange into your experience gradually, then add little pops of yellow.

Maybe the only piece of yellow in your life will be a yellow pencil. That's perfect - it will help you focus!

IMPLEMENTING IT INTO YOUR LIFE

Of all the colors I teach, my clients most quickly jump to yellow. I think it's because people respond to it the quickly online. It draws major attention to any business and can make a very positive impact on the brand and even on sales in some cases.

When it comes to implementing yellow into your life, I'd break it down into sections.

Do I need this lift at home, at work or traveling?

Where does it feel too stimulating? It may be a color that won't work well in your home because it brings too much energy and hyperactivity, but it may be a great fit for your cubicle or outfit to give you energy throughout the day. You may even want to get a dawn-simulating light for your desk.

One of my favorite ways to appreciate yellow is lemons. Undoubtedly, it's my favorite smell in the world. Want me to smile? Let me smell a lemon.

I had a lemon tree grow back from a stump in my youth that created the best smelling lemons I've ever experienced. I miss it terribly! It's easy for me to use lemon as an essential oil in a diffuser, sliced up in my bath or in ice water. It's a way I'm not only seeing yellow, but experiencing it with my other senses.

Remember, this color is designed to lift you up and bring joy into your experience. It may feel foreign, even undeserved. Let color do what it was designed to do by the gift of light and move you through negative emotions and into positive ones.

There's a reason yellow stimulates the emotions and helps you see yourself in the future.

Yellow is usually the color that makes people the most reflective. Most have come to this book with such little knowledge about it so it's surprising! We associate yellow with joy, but this color activates the mind as well.

It can bring a feeling of happiness, but also a feeling of stress in certain cases.

Undoubtedly, this color encourages people to move forward. Not to actually move, that's red. Yellow shows us which direction to move: forward. Towards hope. A brighter future. A sunnier day.

This is why yellow is such a vital color to use in color communication.

Remember yellow on the darkest day. Over the past year, this is now what color flower I always send when someone loses a loved one. To send my thoughts but also, my hope for them to see the sun again as they heal.

What are your thoughts? Can yellow bring more forward momentum to your daily life? Will you start using it in small doses to see what changes you feel?

GREEN
THE COLOR OF GROWTH & EVIL

I REMEMBER HEARING people at my high school making fun of tree huggers, especially around elections. If someone was voting independently or for the green party, they were called a "tree hugger".

Fast forward to today and I don't think there's a color I would want in my environment more than the color green.

On a recent podcast, my friend Brian asked me: "If you had to pick one color that the entire world had to be, what would it be?"

"Green." I answered immediately.

"Really? Even the people?", he asked.

"Yep. Even the people. I would want it all green if I could only choose one." I stated it quite emphatically.

You see, up until 2017, I lived in Los Angeles by Warner Brothers Studios.

I wasn't by an ocean and I wasn't in the mountains. I was in the city.

Now, granted, Burbank at least has some trees, but for the most part, the environment is...you guessed it...gray.

And, over the years, fires wiped out more and more of the hills and hiking trails I was used to exploring for much-needed stress relief. It became harder and harder to find an escape. Even if you did, it was filled with so many other people looking for the same thing that I'd usually leave the experience feeling even more maxed out.

You may feel similarly if you live in a city.

When I started visiting Idaho more and more, I couldn't ignore the change in my body.

You see, northern Idaho is filled with two things: lakes and trees.

As I'm writing this on my deck, I'm looking out over a lake that's surrounded by green. Lots and lots of grasses, trees and mountains.

I'd visit as much as I could because I noticed my stress, chronic pains and moods change and improve. I became more and more relaxed, positive and even energetic in this new environment.

Since we're good friends by this point in the book, you know me well enough to know that I definitely had to research why.

Green is the color of nature. Of balance and harmony. As a psychological primary color, it is the balancer between the mind, body and emotions. Green is very reassuring on a primal level. The color itself equals life, so it's seen as restful and harmonious.

It's all about balance - between the mind, body and emotional self.

SCIENCE

Green falls in the middle of the visible light spectrum, so the eye hardly has to make any adjustments when it looks at the color. The color has been recommended to actually reduce eye fatigue. This finally explained why I had such a dramatic positive change when I relocated to a green-filled environment to contrast all the blue light I was getting from online computer work.

Green is a mix of using the colors yellow and blue. Its wavelength resonates between 495–570 nanometers, but the spread can be different in other cultures that associate it with blue as well. It's a *primary* additive color, which means it's one of the three that are used to create every other color. Complimentary colors to green on the color wheel are generally red or magenta.

We see more varieties in the color green than any other color in our environment.

Did you know that no one is born with green eyes? As someone who has green eyes myself, research showed me that my eyes aren't actually green!

Thought of as the world's most rare eye color (less than 2%), all of the magic lies in the *iris*. This is right outside of the pupil. The *iris* controls how much light enters the eye and it contains all of the pigmented cells that determine eye color.

The optical illusion is caused by the combination of an amber or light brown pigmentation in the *stroma* of the cornea. Blue or green tones are seen in the *iris* due to *Rayleigh scattering* of the reflected light. So, in short, the cells inside of the iris (*melanocytes*) have different amounts of melanin pigment - the less they have, the lighter the eye color due to how it reflects.

So the next time you look in the mirror, check out those gorgeous iris' and appreciate all the detail involved in what color they show...even if it's an illusion!

Green and blue are historically the hardest colors to differentiate across cultures. I've seen many instances where squares of colors are all the same green - with only one blue - and the brain cannot see it.

Studies do show that our ability to recognize the color is extremely linked to knowing the word for the color. (See study at the end of this book.)

HISTORY

The word "green" was first recorded in the year Ad 700 coming from the Old English word *grene*. The Latin word, *viritis*, stems from the word *virere*, which means 'to grow'. Pretty much, you can find roots tied to these original names in Germanic, the romance languages, Slavic and even Greek.

Green pigments did not appear in Neolithic cave paintings, but the people did wear clothing dyed green from the birch tree. Certain ceramics from Mesopotamia show people wearing very vivid green, but no one knows how the colors were created.

The Ancient Egyptians used green to symbolize regeneration and rebirth, symbolizing the yearly flooding of the Nile that caused crops to grow. They used the copper mineral *malachite* to create the color. A paintbox with the *malachite* mineral pigment was found inside the tomb of King Tutankhamun.

Because it was so expensive to mine from the deserts of the Sinai, the Egyptians would more commonly combine yellow *ochre* and blue *azurite* to create green for decoration. For clothing, they would dye fabrics yellow with *saffron* and then soak them in blue dye created from the roots of the woad plant.

A green-growing papyrus sprout was the Ancient Egyptian hieroglyph for "green". Their ruler of the underworld, Osiris, was usually painted with a green face. People would use this color as makeup around their eyes - both the living and dead - to protect them from evil.

Moving forward into Ancient Greece, green and blue were mostly considered the same color. The color is rarely found in Greek art, as it was not seen as one of the four classic colors: red, yellow, black or white. Aristotle thought green to be between the black of the earth and white of the water.

This was used until the Romans soaked their copper plates in wine until it turned the color *verdigris*, a green color that appears as the material ages. The Romans saw green as the color of Venus, their goddess of gardens, vegetables and vineyards. They created an earth pigment used in the wall paintings of many of their cities; Pompeii, Herculaneum, Lyon and Vaison-la-Romaine. At the time, there were ten different words in Latin for the varieties of green.

Green dyes could be made from plants such as plantain, nettles, ferns, buckthorn berries, leeks, the alder tree, the ash tree, the digitalis plant, the fraxinus plant or the broom plant, but they washed out quickly.

Finally, in the 16th century, a process of dying fabrics blue with woad, then yellow with yellow-weed created a reliable green dye for clothing.

It's believed that medieval monks used this color for their manuscripts by using the same wine-soaking method of the Romans. They also used *malachite*.

During the post-modern era in Europe, green was most commonly associated with wealth, merchants and bankers (as opposed to red reserved for royalty at that time).

This is why the *Mona Lisa* is dressed in a green outfit!

Painters like Duccio di Buoninsegna started painting faces with a green undercoat to give the pink skin tone a more realistic hue. With time, however, you can imagine what they look like now as the pink has faded!

In 1775, the toxic chemical *arsenite* was invented by Swedish chemist Carl Wilhelm Scheele. Called *Scheele's Green*, this deadly, bright hue became the most popular dye used.

The dye gave off a toxic odor that made many children and women sick from their walls, toys and dresses. It's rumored that Napoleon Bonaparte's death in 1821 was due to his bedroom being painted *Scheele's Green*.

French Impressionists started using *Paris Green* but it was still highly toxic. Some think this caused Claude Monet's blindness. The color wasn't banned until the 1960s. Current green coloring includes *Pigment Green 7, 36* and *50*, all of which are enormously toxic.

Green was closely associated with the romantic movement in literature and art in the 18th and 19th centuries. Goethe, a German poet and philosopher, declared green a restful color to be used in bedrooms. Painters like John Constable and Jean-Baptiste-Camille Corot showcased lush green forests and scenery.

The color then moved into emotional ties in the second half of the 19th century. James McNeill Whistler was one of the first to make green the central element of his depictions of color, including *Symphony in gray and green; The Ocean* which shows ships swirling in a sea of grays, greens and very little blue.

Van Gogh, one of our favorite color-minded artists, gives great insight into the color:

"I sought to express with red and green the terrible human passions. The hall is blood red and pale yellow, with a green billiard table in the center, and four lamps of lemon yellow, with rays of orange and green. Everywhere it is a battle and antithesis of the most different reds and greens." - Vincent van Gogh, in reference to *Bewaren The Night Cafe Painting*

Many artists like Picasso and Van Gogh also were known absinthe drinkers...an alcohol that is green in color.

In 1895, Albert Maignan painted an image of "the green fairy", or absinthe, overtaking a poet.

We can thank Shakespeare, who coined the phrase "green-eyed monster" in his literature, for re-enforcing the duplicitous nature of green.

The word used for green and blue was the same for many Asian languages throughout history: including Chinese, Thai, Japanese and Vietnamese.

Japan now differentiates green, using one word *midori* for 'flourish' or 'grow' and another *guriin* for the English use of the actual color.

BEHAVIOR

Did you know that surgeons wear mainly green or blue scrubs? It's because they are trained to focus on red, so a green uniform minimizes distraction. Green scrubs improve a surgeon's visual acuity and helps them become more sensitive to different shades of red. This is according to John Werner, a psychologist who studied vision at the University of California, Davis.

Scrubs actually used to be white. In the early 20th century, one doctor decided to switch to green. He thought it would be easier on surgeon's eyes. When they wore white, a surgeon's eyes would create a green "after effect" - kind of like a camera flash - after focusing on so much red during surgery. By switching the scrubs to green, the eyes are able to re-set themselves to seeing color correctly when looking up from the surgical table.

Green has been involved in a variety of experiments, proving that it reduces heart rate when walking but elevates it while running. Let me explain. In the red chapter, we talked about the adrenaline the body creates when red is viewed. The blood pressure goes up, the heart rate, pupils dilate, etc. Think of red as visual fuel.

Green creates the opposite. As we exercise in a green environment, we do not have the motivation like we do with red. Our stimulus tells us to relax. Our bodies think that we're having to exert more effort to keep going than we actually are in a green environment, so we tire more easily. Make sense?

An experiment was performed in Italy, called "The Moving Parks Project", where people exercised in green parks. After three months of this, all psychosocial parameters showed improvement: reduced tension, sadness, fatigue and improved energy, serenity and vitality.

I think we can all agree that walking in the woods is preferable to a treadmill. The body loves being surrounded by green - even when on vacation! It helps us relax.

CURRENT CULTURE & RELIGION

When we think of green in current culture, most of us probably think about Ireland.

In America, St. Patrick's Day is a huge celebration...

bringing corned beef and cabbage, green outfits and even green beer. Rumor has it that the color green first came to be associated with Ireland during the *Great Irish Rebellion* of 1641, where military commander Owen Roe O'Neill led the fight waving a green flag. Some, however, say it all comes from the shamrock, which was supposedly used by St. Patrick to describe the Holy Trinity. In the 1790s, green again came to the forefront of the *Society Of United Irishmen* who wore green liberty caps.

The most famous poem that emerged from that time was *The Wearing Of The Green*. I'm sharing this with you because, at the time, the British outlawed the wearing of the color - it was even punishable by death. It becomes much easier to understand the Irish's current pride in the color, what it truly represents to them and why it stands to this day.

In Native American culture, green is a balancing color to help the physical and mental self. Peyote Art uses green objects to represent Mother Nature. This culture focuses heavily on the use of green herbs for medicine, and believe even the color itself has healing abilities.

Green is the color most closely tied to Islam. It is believed Muhammed's robe and banner were green. In the *Quran* (whose binding is also green), those in paradise wear green silk robes. It is now a tradition where Muslim's represent themselves in green colors. Green is also the main color of Islamic calligraphy and a main decorative color for mosques.

In Japan, green is symbolic of nature and calm. One of the most traditional hues of green is called *matcha iro*, which is the color of matcha green tea. Japanese nobility have enjoyed tea parties since the 13th century. By the 15th century, the tea ceremony was born which became extremely popular among the samurai. Many Japanese wear green in their clothing as it is restful. Japan celebrates greenery day because of their love and respect for vegetation and nature. This is on April 29th, Emperor Shoowa's birthday, as he loved nature and natural science.

NATURE

When it comes to green in nature, I wanted to take the opportunity to highlight plants. We already know that they have a very similar living process to us - they absorb sunlight in order to create chlorophyll to live.

And, if you've ever read *The Secret Life Of Plants*, you'll know what I'm talking about when I say that they are electromagnetic beings that communicate just like us.

The biggest difference? We have hormones, they have chlorophyll.

In 1966, CIA interrogation specialist Cleve Baxter attached a lie detector to a *Dracaena* plant to see if the plant would respond. He got very clear readings of human responses like fear and excitement.

If you doubt the true sentience of plants, let me introduce you to Dr. Mancuso, Plant Neurobiologist.

"Plants are extremely good at detecting specific kinds of sounds, for example at 200hz or 300hz ... because they are seeking the sound of running water." -Dr. Stefano Mancuso

He describes plants as intelligent, communicative creatures. They can retain memory for months, sense up to 20 chemicals contained in the soil around them and release chemicals when under duress to ward off predators. Plants can even exude certain scents to attract pollinators.

In a Harvard Science Review, it's clearly stated that plants perceive color. They have at least 11 kinds of *photoreceptors* so they can react to sunlight (we only have 2).

Lastly, I wanted to mention one of my favorite trips when I lived in California: the Sequoia National Forest. I've never seen anything like it. Giant Sequoias reaching to the sky. Vivid red trunks contrasted by dark green leaves and a mossy green floor. They are called the largest living organism on earth.

These plants might be the most fascinating of all. They grow root systems that interweave with each other, creating a kind of neural network that can span hundreds of miles. Although it's the biggest tree, it has some of the shallowest roots. But because of its interlocking with other trees and their root systems, it will not fall down, even in the harshest weather.

Clearly, the green we have is nature is not simply vegetation for animals or ourselves. Plants are aware, communicative and even intelligent creatures.

HEALING

In color medicine, green is very neutral and can harmonize one's polarity if one is too stimulated or depressed. Green lasers are used in surgeries.

Green relieves tension by balancing the cerebrum and stimulating the pituitary gland. When used, the color can bring about regeneration and stabilization for most conditions. Noah Goldhirsh loves bringing green plants to friends who are recovering from illness or surgery to encourage their body to heal quickly.

Going back to chromotherapy, I want to introduce you to

Dinshah Pestanji Ghadiali. He wrote the *Spectro-Chrome Metry Encyclopedia* (1933). This book detailed the exact science of chromotherapy. That, along with *20th Century Scientific Emergence,* showed why and how different color rays have such a wide range of therapeutic effects on the body.

> "The colour bands of spectrograms are produced when a chemical element undergoes a process of combustion or vaporization that accelerates the motion of its atoms. The specific band of colours and dark lines emitted when a certain element is heated, are known as Fraunhauafer lines...the chemical elements are colour compounds...A specific disease thus constitutes a specific imbalance of colour waves and by implication, chemical imbalance." - Ghadiali, *Spectrochrome Metery Encyclopedia.*

It's pretty impossible to deny that color is a very intricate part of the body's optimum function.

Charles Klotsche solidified Ghadiali's theory of *color chemistry* through experimentation. He recommends green whenever you're in doubt of what color would be best for treatment. It's the master color as it's right in the middle of the spectrum. It will balance you if you're too stimulated, bringing calm. Or if you're too down, bringing you up. He has found the color green to vibrate at 584 trillion times per second.

MUSIC

The color green correlates to the musical note "C". We can hear this tone in bells and drums.

FILM

In film, green is seen as the "Split Personality Color" since it can show two different realities: life or decay.

There is so much lusciousness and growth in the jungle of *King Kong*, but the skin of the wicked witch makes us see evil in *The Wizard Of Oz*.

Green can even symbolize an artificial reality like in *The Matrix*.

In the movie *Inside Out*, the character of Disgust is green. Green adorns the villain in *Jingle Jangle*.

Why is it that, overwhelmingly in film and television, we equate green with evil? Since we've studied the history, we know that that Ancient Egyptians equated green with Osiris (death) and that green paint was poisonous for centuries.

Even though many film and color psychologists say that green's evil definition originated with *The Wizard Of Oz*, I disagree. I believe it's rooted in our psyche due to our history. Quite possibly even our DNA.

The *Shape Of Water* tried to adjust this. We feel the foreign, evil hue of the laboratory with many scenes of an artificial green. The main character, Elisa, is even dressed in green. But then we see the earthly green creature in captivity. We want him rescued and put back in his habitat - back to nature. The movie moves us into water, his home, where the true green makes us feel safe again.

Green is crying out for more flexibility and expression in film.

WHY YOU LOVE IT

If you're a lover of green, you are most certainly the heart of your home. It is a very calming color that symbolizes an open heart, independence, peace and regeneration. People who love green are usually very centered, love nature and create the stability and dependability so desperately needed in a home environment.

You are probably drawn to some form of greenery in your neighborhood, cook fresh ingredients and even dabble in natural healing of some sort - be it essential oils or herbs.

Green-lovers are usually very warm, supportive and caring people. They are a steady companion that keeps things balanced and healthy. Usually, they are the most responsible and are the first to notice when there is something off or hurting a loved one. They're also the ones that will work the most quickly to fix it.

I'm sure by this point in the green chapter, you understand why you're so deeply drawn to the color and how it can be life-giving and healing in so many ways. Just like you!

WHY YOU HATE IT

There are a few reasons why this might be your least favorite color. Maybe you were a sickly child and hated how green your skin always looked. Or you live in a region of the world where meat spoils easily and you've had some bad experiences.

You may have seen *The Wizard Of Oz* too young and been very frightened by the Wicked Witch. Or even felt oppressed by the society you grew up in that idolized the color. You may have fought in a war surrounded by jungle and sustained injuries or losses.

Whatever the reason, this would be one of the only colors I would ask you to reconsider. This is because it's the only color that can truly stabilize someone. If you're down it will lift you up. If you're too stressed, it will help you calm.

This color is so tied to nature, which is the key to health, that it can only benefit you. Start small, maybe with just one small plant. Grow from there and see what changes as you gradually incorporate this color into your daily life.

IMPLEMENTING IT INTO YOUR LIFE

When I was redecorating my office, I knew that I had the opportunity to create a space that would support the heavy mental capacity needed on a daily basis. With this knowledge, I decided to make my walls a blue-based gray and all of my accents green.

Green curtains, green artwork, green accent pillows and as many green plants as I could fit into a 100 square foot room. Each morning as I walk in, it smells so fresh and clean. I'll work for a few hours, then get up, stretch and water my plants. Or, if it's been a heavy workday with long hours, I'll go outside and spend a good thirty minutes taking in the trees and lake water.

The color green has become a huge stabilizer in my life and I think you can easily do the same in your home. If nothing else, get plants! Not only will this put more oxygen in your home and purify the air, but you'll get physical benefits every time you see the color. Don't feel limited by light, there are many low light or no light plants you can choose from.

If you can, walk in nature more. If that's not possible, see if you can put it on a wall - maybe in your living space to bring a feeling of rejuvenation and peace.

Take mental notes of the changes you start to see: in your mood, your family, even how friends interact with you. Maybe you'll start seeing your colleagues spend more and more time in your green-accented office.

Then you'll know you're on to something.

Have you ever put your feet in the grass? Or run your hands over moss?

On my worst day, I like to head outside and put my bare feet in the soil. We didn't go into this in the science section, but this practice is called "grounding".

Studies show that walking barefoot on soil or grass reduces cortisol levels, helps people fall asleep faster and reduces inflammation and pain. It can even help wounds heal faster. (See the 2 *National Library of Medicine* studies referenced in the back of this book.)

My point is this. There's no other color in the visible light spectrum as closely tied to our environment that we can actually see and touch than green. This vegetation is designed to interact with us and essentially, help us re-balance ourselves.

Sure, we could do some color light therapy sessions and most likely promote a huge amount of healing in your body. You could even get a lot of these effects from sunbathing in limited time frames. But green is the only color dominant in our daily atmosphere that actively participates through vegetation to help us balance, grow, nourish and heal.

Which is why at the beginning of this chapter I said, if we could only see one color, it would have to be green.

What do you think? Do you have more appreciation for the

plant life around you? Are you maybe going to look into getting a Gardyn to grow indoors or take more walks in your nearby forests?

Green is a vital color in our color communication as it gives us a wide range of intonation when used - for better or for worse. For health or decay. For good or for evil.

BLUE
THE COLOR OF CALM & THE MIND

"Among the ancient elements, blue occurs everywhere: in ice and water, in the flame as purely as in the flower, overhead and inside caves, covering fruit and oozing out of clay." - William Gass, On *Being Blue*

BLUE IS PROBABLY the color I wear the most and, living on a lake, enjoy in my immediate environment. It's known as the world's favorite color because we see it all around us: in the sky and in the water.

What's interesting, however, is that its meaning changes in our spoken language.

"I'm feeling blue" means feeling down or depressed.

Blue is another psychological primary color and it centers on the mental. We interpret it as a more detached, calming and mentally stimulating color. It helps us think, reflect and wake up our minds.

The color blue can be equated with logic, clarity of thought, calm, serenity and reflection. Or it can be seen as aloof, cold, uncaring and entirely cerebral. Blue can help us learn and is fantastic to use in schools to help support students - especially those with attention deficit disorders.

As we learned from the experiments in the *'Red'* chapter with Russian Scientist S.V. Krakov in 1942, viewing blue causes a reduction in blood pressure, pupil dilation and heart rate.

If you'd like to try an at-home experiment, put the color in front of someone like a child or spouse. Watch their reaction. Usually, they will immediately take a long, deep relaxing breath.

So, why does the world love this color so much? Let's find out.

SCIENCE

Blue, of course, is the one of the three colors in the RYB model and RGB color models. It lies between cyan and violet in the visible light spectrum, when we see light with a dominant wavelength of 450-495 nanometers.

Blues with a higher frequency (a shorter wavelength) look more violet, those with a lower frequency (and longer wavelength) look more green. If you want a pure blue? That's smack dab in the middle with a wavelength of 470 nanometers. In terms of replicating that shade, I've found the closest to be hex code #2167ff. Blue's complimentary color is orange.

As we talked about in the *'Color and the Brain'* chapter, our retina has cells that help us understand and process light. The retinal cells that comprise the non-image-forming visual pathway between our eye and our hypothalamus are very sensitive to the shorter wavelengths of light - like blue.

Most distant objects actually appear bluish because of *aerial perspective*, which is the effect the atmosphere has on how an object appears when viewed from a distance. As the distance between yourself and what you see grows, the contrast between that object and the background decreases. That causes the colors to become less saturated and to blend into the background color, which is normally blue.

Why do we see blue in our sky and water? It's due to an effect we talked about earlier called *Rayleigh Scattering*. Meaning that as sunlight passes through our atmosphere, the blue wavelengths scatter more widely as they interact with oxygen and nitrogen molecules. This causes us to see more blue in the sky.

Our seas and lakes appear blue because the water absorbs the longer wavelengths of red and scatters the blue, reflecting blue to our eyes.

Remember that irises are really only brown or black. Blue eyes do exactly what the sky and sea does...it scatters light and reflects the shorter-wavelength blue light.

HISTORY

Blue evolved in different ways using different pigment sources all over the world.

Our modern English word "blue" comes from the Middle English and Old French word *bleu*. Other cultures differentiate light blue from dark blue, or use the same word for blue and green.

Egyptian blue was actually the first artificial pigment created by heating *limestone* mixed with sand, copper (such as azurite or malachite) and *natron* around 2200 BC. It was heated between 1470-1650 degrees Fahrenheit, creating an opaque blue glass. This had to be crushed and combined with thickening agents like egg white to create paint or glaze.

Rumor has it that Cleopatra used powered *lapis lazuli* as eyeshadow.

It was used in tomb paintings to protect the dead in the afterlife, so they say. In 2006, scientists put *Egyptian blue* under fluorescent light and saw that it glowed, showing that the pigments emit infrared radiation. Historians now use this technique to more easily identify colors on ancient artifacts when they aren't visible to the naked eye!

Egyptian blue was used throughout the Roman Empire until the end of the Greco-Roman period between 332 BC - 395 AD.

Now let's talk about *ultramarine*, made from the *lapis lazuli* gemstone. It was imported by the Egyptians from the mountains of Afghaniztan. They did try to make a pigment from it, but failed. It instead created a dull gray that they used for jewelry. In the 6th century, "true blue", from *lapis lazuli*, appeared in Buddhist paintings from Bamiyan, Afghanistan.

It was renamed *ultramarine*, meaning "beyond the sea". This is because it was imported to Europe by Italian traders during the 14th and 15th centuries. Artists in Medieval Europe desired it greatly for its royal blue quality. It was so expensive, however, that it was considered as precious as gold.

The color was reserved for very important work, like the blue robes of the Virgin Mary in *Virgin and Child with Female Saints*, painted by Gérard David. You can reference the painting *Girl with a Pearl Earring*, painted by Johannes Vermeer in 1665, to understand how striking this blue was. Vermeer supposedly put his family in debt to paint it. According to art historians, *The Entombment* by Michelangelo was left unfinished because he couldn't afford to buy more *ultramarine* blue.

In 1709, German druggist and pigment maker Johann Diesbach experimented with creating a new red. Potash - potassium-rich salt from wood ashes - accidentally mixed with animal blood. Instead of red, it created blue. It was named *Berliner Blau*, which evolved into *Prussian Blue*. This color was used by Picasso during his "Blue Period". I find this fascinating since blood is naturally blue until removed from the body. This specific blue became a staple for wallpaper colors in homes at that time. As it was shipped worldwide in the early 1800's, it started to be called *Berlin Blue* and was popular in Japan because the color did not fade like the blue they were using from the dayflower.

Nowadays, we use Prussian Blue in pill form to neutralize metal poisoning.

In the 8th and 9th centuries, *cobalt blue* was used to color ceramics and jewelry, especially in China. In 1802, French chemist Louis Jacques Thénard discovered an alumina-based version that became widespread in France, used by painters such as J. M. W. Turner, Pierre-Auguste Renoir, and Vincent Van Gogh as it was much more affordable than ultramarine.

In 1824, the Societé d'Encouragement offered 6,000 francs to anyone who could create a synthetic *ultramarine*. Two men, Jean-Baptiste Guimet, French chemist, and Christian Gmelin, German professor, submitted their discoveries. The committee gave the prize to Guimet and it was called *French Ultramarine*.

In 1842, English astronomer Sir John Herschel found *Berliner Blue* had a unique sensitivity to light, which could be used to create copies of drawings. These are now called "blueprints".

Navy blue, originally called *marine blue* was adopted as the official color of British Royal Navy Uniforms in 1748. This spread to most Navy branches of military worldwide, who have darkened their uniforms to almost blue-black to keep the color from fading.

What we now enjoy everyday in our blue jeans, *indigo*, was synthetically created by German chemists in 1878. This replaced the natural production of indigo which was extracted from plant leaves from the *Indigofera* genus.

Blue was brought into royal fashion by Louis IX of France. The blue suit we now commonly wear had its debut in England in the 17th century. In the 19th century, we saw blue become the uniform for the workforce along with the blue jean (which was named after French "Blue de Génes", for the seaport where the indigo was shipped, named Genoa).

In the mid-1900's, French artist Yves Klein developed a matte version of *ultramarine*, which he coined *International Klein Blue*. Between 1947-1957, he trademarked the color and used it in over 200 works of art.

Most recently, in 2009, a new shade of blue was discovered by Professor Mas Subramanian and his student Andrew E. Smith at Oregon State University. The combination of yttrium, indium and maganese - experimented with to make electronics - turned bright blue when heated. They named it *YInMn blue*, which was released for public use in 2016. You can see it now in the Crayola crayon collection.

BEHAVIOR

There's a room in the United Kingdom that can be turned into any color. Hosted at University of Leeds, this room can be tuned to specific wavelengths in the visible light spectrum. So unlike other lights that use the RGB model by mixing colors together, this room uses specific wavelengths - a much closer replica to sunlight.

They have tested colors like red, green, yellow, magenta

and blue; and blue was found to definitely have the biggest impact with decreasing heart rate.

The behavioral research on blue is fascinating as so many studies have found it to decrease violence and self-harm. Experiments have been performed all over the world; Japan, Scotland, and the United States.

Since the 1990's, college campuses have installed "Blue Light" call boxes so students can call for help in an emergency situation. They've also been put on freeways, bridges, tunnels, parks and parking lots. Rice University in Houston, Texas found that implementing a Blue Light system dropped burglaries by 67%.

In Japan, blue LED lamps were installed on railway platforms. Suicides by jumping in front of trains was extremely high in Japan. This phenomenon was studied by comparing the number of deaths before and after blue lights were installed at 14 different stations. Analysis showed that the number of suicides decreased by 74% at these newly lit stations. They even monitored nearby stations to make sure deaths did not increase there, and they didn't!

Glasgow, Scotland changed their street lighting to blue, supposedly for aesthetic reasons, and noticed a crime drop as well.

It's fascinating that behavior changes are so wildly noticeable here in regards to crime. As we know, blue reduces heart rate and blood pressure. It can even calm someone's mood. We know it engages the mind and can bring someone into a much more reflective state.

Could color psychology explain the stark difference in violent crimes?

Let's pivot to other behavior effects from the color blue. The University of Basel in Switzerland found that exposure to blue light affected athletes ability to compete. Since most games happen at night, they wanted to see if blue light exposure made any difference in their performance.

Since blue light reduces the production of *melatonin*, the sleep hormone, it's no surprise that it significantly improved the athletes' performances when tested.

It's also worth noting that blue light (400-500 nm) is most damaging to the retina. As we do so much computer and LED work nowadays, many have gotten blue-light blocking glasses to wear when they are in front of a screen or under LED lights to protect their vision.

CURRENT CULTURE & RELIGION

The color blue is a staple of Judaism. In the Torah, the Israelites were commanded to interweave blue into the fringes of their garments. They akin the color to God's glory as Ezekiel and Exodus describe the "pavement of sapphire" as well as the Ten Commandments which were said to be made of sapphire stone.

The *Mishkan* - the portable tabernacle of Yahweh - contained items such as the menorah and the Ark of the Covenant, which were covered in blue cloth when moved from place to place while wandering the wilderness. (Numbers 4:6-12)

Blue is used for *Hannukah* decorations, and clothing called *tekhelet* is dyed with indigo. The Star of David, an iconic symbol of the Jewish faith, is also blue.

In Hinduism, blue is tied to many deities. Krishna is blue, embodying love and joy. Rama is also blue, seen as a protector of humanity.

Chinese and Tibetan cultures revere blue, seeing it as a

color to be respected. Their holy texts were written in dark blue ink.

Blue is also seen in Christianity, Sikhism and Paganism.

Since blue is seen as a harmonious color, we see it in the flags of the United Nations and European Union. The United States has associated this color with the democratic party for many decades.

We see it used mainly in the technology industry worldwide. Since it's the color of communication and clarity, it's easy to understand why most social media platforms have embraced it. The phrase "true blue" comes from something being one hundred percent dependable, like the blue sky. Subconsciously, we think of these companies as more dependable and trustworthy.

NATURE

Blue is very rare in nature outside of the sky and the water. Less than 10% of the world's nearly 300,000 species of flowers are blue. Even less have blue leaves - except for a few plants found on the floor of tropical rainforests.

A flower or leaf appearing blue would mean a plant reflects the color, absorbing the rest. With blue it would be extremely unlikely, since plants readily absorb blue light due to its high amounts of energy. Most plants absorb blue light to use in their internal processes because they need it for photosynthesis. This is unlike green, where plants appear green because chlorophyll reflects green light.

We talked about *lapis lazuli* earlier, and this rare mineral contains *trisulfide* ions - three sulfur atoms tied together inside a crystal lattice - that have the ability to bind or release a single electron. That energy difference creates the blue we see in the mineral.

What's wild is that animals do not get their blue coloring from chemical pigments. They actually manipulate light. For example, the *Morpho* butterfly genus have layered nanostructures on their wings that take layers of light and only reflect blue. A similar effect happens with the feathers of the blue jay, the scales of blue tang fish and the rings of the blue-ringed octopus.

Blue fur is not naturally a vivid color. The platypus, for example, is not blue in visible light. Certain species glow blue under ultraviolet light, like the platypus. Otherwise, we see blue with some whale species, poison dart frogs, certain dolphins, and specific monkeys and mandrills.

There's quite a mystery with blue, as most food companies are still on the hunt for a natural food dye source so they can ditch the *Brilliant Blue SCF* they currently use. They're specifically looking at flowers for this possibility, as the most brilliant and concentrated blue colouration of any living tissue is in the marble berries of the *Pollia condensata* found in the forested regions of Africa. If you can, look it up because it is absolutely stunning!

We also do no see any blue food - the commonly called blueberry is actually purple.

HEALING

Blue is an interesting healing color, since we know so much of it resides within the mind.

Avicenna found blue to reduce blood flow, cooling inflamed conditions.

Pleasanton, author of *19th Century Ideas and Practices*, focused on blue in his studies. He said blue was the first remedy to use with burns, aches or injuries to reduce inflammation. Experiments showed that blue light exposure could 'cure' certain diseases, increase fertility and cause animals to fully mature in less time. In 1999, Hassan continued the use of blue in burn treatments and injuries as well.

Chromotherapy advocate Edwin Babbitt further used blue for inflammatory conditions, headaches, nerves, irritability, sunstroke, meningitis and even sciatica. Robert Gerard found that physical exposure to cooler colors calmed anxiety, tension, reduced blood pressure, alleviated muscle spasms and aided insomnia.

When used in color medicine, Klotshe states that blue can increase the elimination of toxins. It can provide more restful sleep while also activating the pineal gland. He has found blue to vibrate at 658 trillion times per second.

Until the 1960s, risky blood transfusions were the only way neonatal jaundice could be treated. A few years before, studies had suggested that sunlight exposure (artificially replicated with full-spectrum light) was a successful treatment. Blue light was soon found to be even more effective and less hazardous - effectively treating the condition.

All of this research shows that using blue may assist in bringing down anxiety, heart rate, blood pressure and high emotional states. It almost seems too simple that this effect could be achieved by simply seeing the color blue!

MUSIC

The color blue correlates to the musical note "D". Not surprisingly, we hear this tone in the ocean waves. Indigo, blue's cousin, correlates to "D#" which we can hear from bees.

FILM

In film, blue is "The Detached Color". It's very useful in a variety of ways on-screen; it can be used to quiet oneself, grieve, or even emotionally remove us from an event.

> "There's a great story about Knute Rockne, the famous Notre Dame football coach, who, back in the 1920s, painted his visitors locker rooms blue and won every game season after season. Theory is, he totally spaced out his opponents with blue and fired up his own team with red." - Patti Bellantoni, *If It's Purple, Someone's Gunna Die*

You'll see this color used specifically in scenes that appear harsh (like winter in *The Revenant*) or even forced calm (like *The Truman Show*).

> "Blue can be a tranquil pond or a soft blanket of sadness. It is quiet and aloof. Year after year, our color investigations show that in a blue environment, people become passive and introspective. It's a color to think to, but not to act." -Patti Bellantoni, *If It's Purple, Someone's Gunna Die*

You can also see this in *Jurassic World* with the raptor character, 'Blue'. The other raptors are a mixture of greens and yellows, pretty close to what reptilians naturally have in their skin pigment. Even red would have been an evolutionary understandable choice. So why is 'Blue', blue?

You may say it's because of her name. However, she was named with military names, like her sisters Charlie, Delta and Echo (she would have been named Bravo in this case). Blue is the only one in the series with advanced intelligence and empathy who has a relationship of trust with the main character, Owen. This explains why they chose the color blue.

WHY YOU LOVE IT

If you are a lover of Blue, you are probably a very intelligent person. You may even be thought of as the most introspective of your social group. Wanting to mull things over, you think before you act and usually before you speak. You enjoy slowing things down to have time to process and love a nice calming atmosphere.

Rare to get too emotional or heated, you like to keep your atmosphere calm and for things to make sense. It's easy for you to maintain relationships where there is clear communication - hot heads tend to make you pull away.

Blue in your environment always brings a feeling of peace and you like to put it on your skin to keep you level throughout the day.

WHY YOU HATE IT

Blue may absolutely repel you if you are not someone that likes to think deeply or spend much time by yourself. It's rare as it's the world's favorite color, but some people spend so much of their workday in their heads that they do not want blue anywhere in their environment.

You also may want to be more in the moment, more emotional, more expressive - and blue feels like a color that pulls you down. Your instincts may even tell you to stay away from your phone at night, especially since blue light reduces the ability to fall asleep.

Whatever the reason, hopefully the breakdown of this chapter has helped you appreciate what the color can do when used under the right circumstances.

IMPLEMENTING IT INTO YOUR LIFE

This is an easy color to start putting into your life. Start by figuring out which aspects of your routine and home need a bit more calm.

For example, maybe your office has been yellow and it's too stimulating. Painting it blue may help you stay on-task. But be cautious: in some cases, the wall color can put people to sleep!

Maybe you feel way too stressed when exercising at home while doing a low-impact activity. Try putting some blue in the environment to see if it becomes more restful for you.

A lighter blue will feel more soothing. The darker and more saturated the blue, the more mentally-driven it will become.

No matter what, however, it will always evoke a strong mental reaction - whether it's calming or concentrative.

I like to focus blue into my living environment because, as a Type A person, I need more calming tones in my home and office. This may be too suppressive to other personality types but for me, it helps me reduce stress. Some touches I have are blue rugs, blue cabinets and a blue couch.

As I'm sure you can see, there is a ton of history, research and even peculiar displays in nature concerning the color blue. I thought it would be the easiest color to write, but it has definitely been the most complex in terms of defining the color as there are so many shades, hues, tints and tones.

My appreciation for this color has grown as history demonstrates how deeply people yearned for it in their clothing, artwork and expression. They were willing to pay as much as they would for gold!

Color is truly precious and a needed element to communicate, especially with clarifying thoughts.

Maybe we so deeply love blue because of its historical rarity...or because we are surrounded by a blue sky and blue water.

Whatever the reason may be, blue has earned its name as the world's favorite color in my opinion and is an essential tool for communication in our daily life.

PURPLE
THE COLOR OF CONNECTION & SPIRITUALITY

"I think it pisses God off if you walk by the colour purple in a field somewhere and don't notice it." -Alice Walker, *The Color Purple*

PURPLE CAN BE the most challenging color in every area.

From wearing it, to having it be in a brand, to existing in someone's home.

People are very unsure about purple.

It can make you feel contemplative, reflective, spiritual and even mystical. But it can also make you out of touch with reality and come across as cheap.

Purple is an extremely strong color to work with that I think can hit people the hardest - in a good way but also easily a bad one.

Ultimately? We connect when we see purple.

I purposefully wear it anytime I'm meeting someone new or going to a family gathering.

Maybe I'd wear blue if I was speaking or hosting a meeting online. For a one on one connection? I'd wear purple.

I've named this chapter *'Purple'*, but we will be covering

both purple and violet here. Keep in mind that violet is the color in the visible light spectrum and the rainbow, purple is a man-made color.

SCIENCE

Purple is created by combining red and blue. Remember that blue is the mental psychological primary and red the physical. Red brings power, energy and strength, while blue brings integrity, truth and reasoning. Used together they create purple, connecting the mental and physical, which is why it can be seen as a spiritual and mystical color.

In the visible light spectrum, we see violet - not purple - which is why I use the terms interchangeably in this chapter. Violet's name comes from the violet flower.

Violet is on the shorter end of the visible spectrum, resting between 380-450 nanometers between blue and ultraviolet light (a wavelength past our vision).

Violet has the shortest wavelength, so it's the last color we see in the light spectrum before ultraviolet. This is why people associate it with creating connections with a higher realm.

Purple is a *non-spectral color,* since we don't see it in the rainbow and the color we know purple to be is a man-made creation combining red and blue. For us to see purple, red and blue signals are sent to the brain and, depending on the combination, our brains interpret the color as purple. Unlike other colors listed in this book, purple does not correspond to a specific type of electromagnetic radiation as it is not a spectral color.

Painters find purple between the coloring of violet and crimson. On the color wheel, however, it's placed between violet and magenta, called *electric purple*. The complementary color to violet is yellow.

We don't see a lot of violet in man-made creations because it is so dark to our vision. It can even appear a bit reddish due to how our cones interpret it.

Monochromatic violet light can't be produced by the RGB color system that we use with screens, but it can be approximated by tricking the eye with a strong blue primary color and a weak red primary color. They are able to produce what looks like a short-wavelength violet color out of combining light with two longer wavelengths.

The easiest way to understand the difference between the two colors is brightness. As violet colors brighten, they look more blue. Purple does not do that, it turns more red. This effect is called the *Bezold-Brücke shift* or *luminance-on-hue effect*. All it means is that as a light intensity changes, there's a change in hue perception by our eye. If they are below 500 nm, they will become more and more blue (like with violet). If they are above 500 nm, they will become more and more yellow. This can only happen with colors in the visible light spectrum.

HISTORY

The term for violet came late to languages. It derives from the Old French word *violet* or *violete*. One of the first written records of the term in English comes from the mid-14th century from The Duke of John Maundeuill: *"Men fynd dyamaundz of violet colour"* (*"Men find diamonds of violet colour"*).

Purple was found in cave drawings in the Neolithic era, made from minerals like manganese and hematite. This is still used today by the Aranda people (indigenous Australians) and Hopi Indians (Arizona) for rituals.

Western Polynesians created violet from sea urchins and in Central America, they made violet dye from *purpura* snails. Even the Mayans used this color for their religious ceremonies and the Aztecs used it for their ideogram paintings, symbolizing royalty.

The Ancient Greeks and Hebrews used purple moss, called *orcein*.

A fascinating production of violet is from the dye produced by crushing the *spiny dye-murex* snail. This dye came to be known as *Tyrian Purple* in 15th century BC as it was used in art in the coastal town of Tyre on the coast of ancient Phoenicia (rumored to translate to 'land of purple').

The color became associated with royalty, most likely due to its intensive process to make, among kings, priests, magistrates and even the Hebrew Bible. Tens of thousands of snail glands had to be boiled for ten days or more and wool garments dipped into it for five hours at a time and dried. This was repeated until they achieved the right tone of color. Black-purple was much more favorable than red-purple at the time.

In Exodus, the color *purpura* - Latin for *Tyrian Purple* - is commanded to be used in the curtains of the Tabernacle and priests garments. In the early Christian Era, the gospels were mainly written with gold ink on *Tyrian Purple* parchments!

Empresses gave birth in a room named the 'Purple Chamber' so that emperors born there were said to have been "born to the purple", meaning they naturally held the title by birth and did not seize it.

Alexander the Great wore *Tyrian Purple* as well as the basileus (monarchs) of the Seleucid Empire and the kings of Ptolemaic Egypt.

The color is also referenced in the *Iliad of Homer* and the

Odyssey.

Why was purple so special to Rome? Historically, only the wealthiest men (with more than 400,000 secterces) were inducted into a special class called the *equites*. This gave them permission to wear *Tyrian purple*.

You've heard of the toga, right? We picture it as a white robe over one shoulder. Traditionally, a purple stripe was always around the border of it. The fancy toga? All purple with gold embroidery that the generals and magistrates wore.

It became such a precious color in the eyes of royalty that Nero made certain purple dyes illegal to be used. In fact, in the late empire, selling purple cloth outside of certain royals was punishable by death! Some sneaky manufacturers tried using indigo as a substitute for *Tyrian purple,* but they were heavily punished as well. Julius Ceasar also attempted to "own" the color by ruling that only senators could wear it daily and others could only wear purple on certain days of the year.

Now we understand in the Hebrew New Testament why it was so out of the ordinary for the Romans to dress Christ in purple at that time, even thought it was a mockery of his station before crucifixion. (Mark 15:17 and 20)

Fast-forward to 2008. German Chemist Friedander worked to recreate this incredible *Tyrian purple* known for its richness and durability. He used 12,000 snails to produce 1.4 ounces of dye...which was enough to color one single handkerchief.

China was the first country to produce a synthetic alternative to purple, as they had previously used the purple *gromwell* plant which was very challenging for garments to absorb. It was well-favored in the state of Chi between 1046-221 BC because its ruler enjoyed the color. Its original dye was named *Han Purple.*

Here's the interesting part. Ancient China had 5 prized colors: red, blue, yellow, black and white. Purple used to be tied to impropriety while red was linked to good fortune, joy and legitimacy. By the 6th century, however, purple overran red in the eyes of the people.

Now, China associates purple with love, divinity and immortality.

Let's fast-forward to why the royal popularity of the color purple was crushed, which happened in 1453. Constantinople fell to the Ottoman Turks and purple lost its imperial status as the colors of the new power were green and red.

A few years later, in 1464, the head of the Catholic Church Pope Paul II decreed that cardinals must move their colors from purple to scarlet. This pretty much destroyed any further use of *Tyrian purple*, as future cardinals and university teachers wore purple sourced from indigo thereafter.

When Henry Howard, the Earl of Surrey, was tried for high treason against Henry VIII in 1547, part of the evidence against him was that he had been seen wearing purple. At the time, only the king was allowed to wear it.

During the Elizabethan era, Queen Elizabeth I had strict laws on what colors, fabrics and clothes could be worn by different classes in society. This included only the close relatives of the royal family being allowed to wear purple.

We see the use of purple transfer to more of the spiritual aspect with Renaissance paintings featuring angels and the Virgin Mary in the color.

There was quite a worldwide hunt for violet synthetic dyes in the 18th century.

- *Cudbear*: extracted from *orchil* lichens for dying wool and silk, developed by Dr. Cuthbert Gordon of Scotland in 1758.
- *French Purple*: extracted from lichen through ammonia developed in France around the same

time as *Cudbear*.

- **Cobalt Violet**: made by a similar process to cobalt blue and most commonly used by artists today
- **Mauveine/Aniline Purple/Perkin's Mauve**: the first synthetic organic chemical dye discussed below.

Soonafter, *Tyrian purple* made a royal comeback with Catherine the Great. Other people of status wore it as well, but it was not available to most due to its high cost.

When did the public finally gain access to synthetic *Tyrian purple*? Funnily enough, when eighteen year old British chemistry student William Henry Perkin came on the scene in 1856. His goal? To make synthetic quinine to treat malaria. What happened? The first synthetic dye that looked like the color *mauve* (the name was taken because it was the same shade as the *mallow* flower).

Queen Victoria made the color famous by wearing it to the Royal Exhibition of 1862. Perkin saw his opportunity and built a factory to supply the color by the ton. This had a huge impact and takeover of not only the fashion industry but the chemical industry as well!

In the 19th century, *Orcein* purple became popular again as it was common for demi-mourning - the color worn after black before transitioning to regular colors during the grieving process.

English royalty continued to favor the color through George VI and Elizabeth II - who had it prominently displayed at her coronation in 1953.

Then purple changed. It shifted for the first time in history to the political instead of the royal, becoming the primary color of the Women's Suffrage movement, starting in New York in 1848 - which continued through 1917.

Then it sought to differentiate religious views of Jehovah's Witnesses in concentration camps in Germany, where prisoners wore a purple triangle.

Further, it became tied to psychedelics, drugs and alternative lifestyles in the 1960s-1970s through songs like *Purple Haze* and *Purple Rain*.

BEHAVIOR

Purple, similar to Orange, is not a heavily researched color when it comes to influencing behavior. Most of the studies I could find were done with children.

A *Frontiers In Psychology* study wanted to see how changing a very well-known childhood game, "Red Light, Green Light" to "Red Light, Purple Light" would affect children's performance during their coming preschool year. Evidence showed improvements in math scores and even self-regulation. Something as small as a game tweak helped children engage and develop further in regards to their ongoing education, which was quite remarkable.

In one of the rare adult studies by *Academia* relating colors to moods, purple made people feel relaxed and calm. The positive associations of purple were mainly of children and laughing, while the negatives were simply that it wasn't a favorite color. *Psychology Today* polls echo this, showing that women listed purple as one of their top-tier colors, whereas men did not rank it at all.

Even though this is a relatively untested color, I've been able to use my personal experiences to study it.

I wore purple to write this chapter and its the most lightheaded I've felt writing the entire book! This was interesting as we've seen so many references to it being the most short-wave frequency color tied to the non-corporeal.

With clients and students, this is a business brand color that usually only comes up with women. I have one male client who has decided to trust me with using it, but we've chosen a more blue-based purple.

Audiences see it as a spiritual color. I've had doulas, relationship therapists, spiritual counselors and even life coaches choose this as their primary branding color because it connects with their target client incredibly well.

CURRENT CULTURE & RELIGION

The United States coined September *National Recovery Month* in 1989 and gave it the color purple. It's since expanded to also include the addiction recovery movement. People put up purple signs, fireworks, purple lights and decorations to dedicate memory to those who have lost their lives to addiction. Purple is meant to be a visual cue to celebrate the people who have chosen to recover and to expand awareness of the movement.

A color of honor, the United States also gives the military's highest award, called the *Purple Heart*. It's only given to a service member who has greatly sacrificed themselves, or given their life in the line of duty.

Thailand has an interesting relationship with the color purple. The 500 Baht note is light purple in color. Most Thai airlines use purple on their planes. Thailand is also the only country that assigns specific colors to wear on certain days of the week. Purple is to be worn on Saturdays as it is the color of Shani, the Hindu god of justice and is linked to the planet

Saturn. It is also the color for widows to wear while mourning, while other mourners must wear black.

Her Royal Highness Princess Maha Chakri Sirindhorn, third child of the King and Queen of Thailand, was born on a Saturday. That made purple her birth color, so it is the color of her royal standard when she attends events. You will see purple flowers, flags and backgrounds of her photos in purple.

In Guatemala, Catholics celebrate Easter as *Holy Week* by reenacting the days leading up to Christ's crucifixion and resurrection. On Good Friday, men and boys dress in purple robes and hoods as a sign of mourning and a symbol of the pain and suffering of Christ.

Brazil also has many devout Catholics who wear purple, along with black, to grieve a loved one. It can even be considered disrespectful to wear the color outside of a funeral as it has such sacred, devotional meaning.

I'm sure you're having a much deeper understanding of the spiritual link to purple by now - as I did - as the tie to the noncorporeal becomes so clear by its use around the world.

NATURE

We see purple in nature mostly in plants, who make a group of chemicals called anthocyanins. Think violets, lavender, pansies, crocuses, irises, lupine, snapdragon and nightshade.

Mammals cannot create natural pigments for green, blue or purple. Certain birds and insects can show purple through something called *structural colouration*. This means the tiny scales of butterflies and beetles, or the structures in bird feathers reflect light a certain way to appear purple, like we discussed earlier.

The occasional sea slug, coral, aubergine plant, sea star and purple honeycreeper bird are where we mainly see purple in wildlife.

HEALING

I find Noah Goldhirsh's reflections on purple to be most fascinating. She states that it teaches us "gratitude for all the good in our lives, enabling us to see things differently, come to terms with our life lessons, to heal and close cycles in our lives." Considering it a supportive color, she also adds that it can help us identify and end negative relationships.

She recommends it for children to increase their capacity for gratitude and to help them complete tasks.

With color medicine, both purple and violet can be used, but not in the same way.

Purple can calm the emotions as well as activity in the arteries, Klotshe has found. It can relieve pain in the head and lower blood pressure. The color can slow down overactive kidney and adrenal glands. He has found purple to vibrate at 621 trillion times per second.

What about violet?

It is a cooling color, according to Klotshe, that calms the metabolic process. Violet relaxes the muscles, builds the spleen and calms the lymph glands. It's a great color to soothe and bring on sleep. He has found violet to vibrate at 731 trillion times per second.

If you really want to do a deep dive on color therapy, I highly recommend Kirlian photography. This was invented by Kirlian in 1939, where he found that if an object on a photographic plate is subjected to a high voltage electric field, an image is made. It looks like a colored halo or even a coronal discharge, said to be the physical manifestation of the electromagnetic radiation surrounding the body. I've had it done a couple of times and the results have been fascinating!

Before we leave healing, I'd like to introduce you to M. Hassan. He is a fellow chromotherapist, joining the others we've learned of so far, but he did something really interesting. Not only did he study color, he also defined the electromagnetic transfer of color characteristics. He measured the production of a 32 su (sparkle units) charge in chromotized water due to the absorption of rays. Unfortunately, this has not been further studied, but it does show the movement from chromotherapy to hydrochromotherapy, which introduces the component of water.

Even more stunning are his reflections on color being used and created by the body.

"An electric charge is produced due to the influence of the vibrations of cosmic and colourful rays upon the brain cells. This electric charge takes the form of a current emitted where various cells collide with another. This collision results in formation of incalculable colourful vibrations, which can be termed as thought." - Hassan M. Chromopathy. Peshawar: Institute of Chromopathy; 2000.

Isn't that interesting? Color influencing our brain cells. Our thoughts creating color vibrations. The body communicating and operating around one focal point: color.

MUSIC

The color purple correlates to the musical note "E". We hear this tone when we meditate and say "om".

FILM

In film, purple is called the "Beyond The Body Color".

"There seemed to be no real evidence of purple's having an effect in the physical realm at all. The color did, however, hold a powerful sway in the realm of the noncorporal, the mystical, and even the paranormal." -Patti Bellantoni, *If It's Purple, Someone's Gunna Die*

We would think that purple would have the strongest associations with royalty due to its history. Polls show that audiences, however, tie purple to the spiritual ten times more than the royal.

Movies like *West Side Story, The Sixth Sense, Gladiator + Chicago* use purple to symbolize a character's impending death. Or that something is coming to shake their reality.

This can be easily seen in the *Avengers* movie with Thanos' character, whose skin is purple. He literally symbolizes the coming death of half the population of the planet as well as the mysticism of the infinity stones.

An interesting aside is the name of Tyrion Lanister in *Game of Thrones*. Could this have been a nod to the royal status of his name? Or alluding to his future as hand of the king?

If you watched *The Good Place*...did you notice the AI Janice character was in a purple dress? And the architect, Michael, wore purple in a lot of episodes? These two characters clearly symbolize the afterlife and the huge twist the foursome will soon discover.

WHY YOU LOVE IT

If you love purple/violet, you are probably the most spiritual person you know. Intellectuals or the overly-passionate are usually not attracted to the color.

But, you will see it used when any personality is trying to become more spiritual and connected.

Purple-lovers want to know more about the mystical. They love mysteries, exploration and spiritual studies. This a color loved by someone who is, in a word: open. They want to see, experience and explore above anything else.

People may call you "woo", but you couldn't care less. You're drawn to stones, prims and any type of energy healing - including reiki, meditation, sound therapy, breath work and prayer.

Don't let others underestimate you. Use your strengths of spirituality and intuition to encourage understanding and try to speak your discoveries in ways that someone can understand practically.

WHY YOU HATE IT

If you hate purple/violet, you might have been raised by hippies. No joke, the overly "far out, man" peace movement may have seemed absolutely impractical to you, especially if you're a blue or red personality.

People who hate purple usually tie the color to the paranormal, mystical or dark magic side of things. We've seen through history, however, that those ties are not true.

Try focusing on the spiritual side outside of modalities you're uncomfortable with. For example, start by getting a lavender plant. Look at it once a day and see how it makes you feel after a week.

Our goal is to always, always confront our negative bias with specific colors using all sides of our brains and bodies:

- Physical: show our bodies there is nothing to fear with the color and that our aversion is not truly physically-based
- Emotional: analyze our negative experiences with the color and detach from the negative association by creating positive experiences to balance it
- Mental: strategize ways the color could actually bring assistance into our lives
- Spiritual: understand that the color is designed, along with all of the others in the spectrum, to assist us in every aspect of life

In most cases, an aversion to color is due to bias (culture, trauma, trusted opinions) or imbalance (our body is out of balance and is repulsed by the color it needs).

IMPLEMENTING IT INTO YOUR LIFE

In this case, I recommend the use of violet in your environment and not purple. As purple is a man-made color, no true physical benefit will be enjoyed by its use outside of specific color light therapy. Violet, however, will.

The easiest way to find violet is floral, so try to find places to display these flowers throughout your home. This is a great way to decorate your garden or even a windowsill so that you can start viewing the color on a daily basis.

You can also start finding more violet-shaded clothing,

artwork or furniture. Be careful, however, as too much violet in our environment can make us feel spacey.

To use purple, this is easier to do when it comes to our clothing. The main purpose of our use of this color is twofold - to connect more deeply in our relationships and to open ourselves up spiritually.

Keep this in mind as you attend family gatherings, go on dates, deal with a tense friendship or even try to re-connect with a grown child. You hold the true power here, of course, but the color can aid your intentions.

Violet and purple have certainly been a wild ride, haven't they? There's so much depth of understanding with these two colors that it almost makes us want to step away and take a nap to recharge.

It is not a color found in large supply in our natural environment, and I'm sure that's because it's a light spectrum color our bodies - and other animals - must need for optimum function.

What I enjoy most about this color is that it's the only one that truly supports us spiritually. To me, that reinforces that we are not just physical beings, which red supports. Or just emotional, which yellow supports. And certainly not just mental, which blue supports. We are spiritual as well, an aspect of our design that requires its own spectral support with violet.

That fact encourages me, knowing these colors all exist within our world for a reason. Which, incidentally, proves that we are all here at this designated time, for a reason.

And that is a reassuring thought.

PINK/MAGENTA
THE COLORS OF COMFORT & REVOLUTION

You may be wondering why I'm even bothering with this color, since it's not in the visible light spectrum.

Funnily enough, when I was on the TEDx stage talking about color in 2018, I had someone approach me at intermission. He came right at me and practically yelled, "What about MAGENTA?!".

I'd also had dozens of business owners telling me pink caused an emotional reaction with their audiences.

Obviously, this wasn't a color I could keep ignoring.

It may not be a visible light spectrum color, but for multiple reasons, it does cause a reaction in the body and clear behavioral responses. We'll outline how in this chapter.

I do want to note - there is a very clear distinction of meaning between the colors pink and magenta. They are completely different in how they are created in the brain, how we respond to them and even how they're used in film.

Ready to learn about the *Battle of Magenta* and pink prisons?

SCIENCE

Let me get nerdy for a second.

If I were to say that color is the same as frequency, which is the same as music...would you consider me nuts? Hopefully not by this point.

It isn't far from the truth when it comes to breaking down color scientifically. Color is simply how our brains perceive a wavelength. How we "see" a frequency.

We all remember that our eyes are made up of *photoreceptor* cells called rods and cones, from the beginning of the book, right? Rods detect light and cones distinguish colors between red, green and blue. Every color we see is some type of combination. As we look at the rainbow - red, orange, yellow, green, blue, indigo, violet - we associate each color with the frequency or wavelength it corresponds to.

For example, yellow is a blend of red and green cone reactions. When we see yellow, our brain says, "hey, that's a combination of red and green, so this is what yellow looks like."

The hangup is that magenta and pink do not have a frequency or wavelength.

The color itself lies between red and blue. As we see in the rainbow, however, magenta/pink does not appear between them. Our brain makes up the color in some cases.

Pink

Pink is seen as a light red color - especially since red and white combine to create the shade. It is an *extra-spectral* color as it does not appear in the visible light spectrum. It's complimentary shade is dark green.

Let's go back to sunsets. Why do we see pink in the sky if it isn't truly a spectral color? The effect is because of our old friend *Rayleigh scattering*. Shorter wavelength colors, like blue and green, scatter more strongly as the sun either appears or disappears, removing them from the light that reaches our eyes. We're left with seeing orange, red and pink light - which remember, the brain invents. Kind of like purple.

As a random aside, did you know the United States based company Owens Corning was the first one to trademark a color? They create pink insulation and trademarked the color in 1985 to prevent competitors from using it!

Magenta

The color of magenta is defined as more of a purpleish-red or reddish-purple. This is because the color, to us, appears between violet and red. Technically, violet and red are on opposite ends of the visible spectrum with completely different wavelengths...so it's a wonder that we see magenta this way.

The RGB and CMYK color wheels place magenta between red and blue. Remember that this is one of the main colors used in printing, along with yellow, black and cyan. In the RGB model, the magenta name is interchangeable with fuchsia, and it made by combining red and blue light in equal amounts at high intensity.

Magenta is an *extra-spectral* color, meaning it is not in the visible light spectrum. Its complementary color is yellow-green.

In the eye, we see magenta as the wavelengths of blue hit

the short wave and long wave cones, but not the middle wave cones.

Astronomers have given T brown dwarfs, a spectral class of stellar classification, the color appointment of magenta due to the absorption by sodium and potassium atoms of light that are in the green portion of the spectrum.

We will use the terms *magenta* and *fuchsia* interchangeably as they are the same color, but referred to as one or the other throughout history.

HISTORY

As the two colors have completely different histories, I will split up pink and magenta throughout the rest of this chapter.

Pink

We get the name *pink* after the *pink* flower. The frilled edges of the flowers led to terms like *pinking shears* and "to pink", which means decorating with a perforated or punched pattern, which dates back to the 14th century.

The color has been in literature since ancient times, seen in the 800 BCE *Odyssey* by Homer, as he refers to the "child of morning, rosy-fingered dawn". *Roseus* was the Latin word used, which meant *rosy* or *pink*.

Most tied to the color of human flesh, pink was not a common color of fashion in the Middle Ages. It was a color associated with the body of Christ. It started appearing in art in the 13th and 14th centuries, especially in works by Duccio and Cimabue.

A popular work, *Madonna of the Pinks* by Raphael, shows

the Christ child giving a pink flower to the Virgin Mary during the high Renaissance.

The pink pigment used for painting people's bodies was *cinabrese*; mixing *sinopia/Venetian red* earth pigment (red) and *Bianco San Genovese* lime pigment (white).

In the 18th century, pink peaked in popularity. This was when pastel colors were extremely fashionable across Europe. The favorite color of Madame de Pompadour, the mistress of King Louis XV of France; she wore it constantly and even had a shade created exclusively for her by the Sèvres porcelain company, whose prized porcelain in this shade came to be associated with the opulence of the royal court.

The double-meaning escalation of pink was firmly established during this time, as it was painted as the color of romance and seduction by certain painters and the color of childhood by others.

In the 19th century, pink was commonly worn by young boys. Since men in England wore red uniforms, the color pink was seen as masculine for male children. Rumor has it that in the 1920's, a US department store production error shipped clothes that were reversed - with boys clothes in blue and girls clothes in pink. They rolled out new advertising, and it stuck!

If you're familiar with air force history in World War II, you probably know about the *Supermarine Spitfire*, a small, one-man fighter plane used by the British Royal Air Force.

If you didn't know, this plane was painted entirely pink.

The planes were needed to fly over the German camps and take photos of what they were up to - so it could be reported back as intelligence for battle plans. These fighters needed to have the ability to make it to their target location, take photos, circle back and return safely.

The Royal Air Force gave the unit flexibility in what they

painted their planes. Many shades were tried, but pink won out. But why?

As they flew under cloud cover, the color would disappear against them. It also was impossible to see at sunrise and sunset.

The paint color used was *Mountbatten Pink*, and it has a history.

In 1940, Lord Mountbatten, a British military officer who was also related to the British Royal family, was escorting a convoy by sea. He had joined the Royal Navy in World War I, so he was very familiar with ships and naval operations.

During this convoy, he noticed something. A companion ship disappeared from view much earlier than the rest. The only difference from the other gray ships? This one was painted lavender mauve gray. If you'd like to look up the shade, it is #997A8D.

He knew this could protect his ships during their most dangerous time, sunrise and sunset, and had his whole fleet painted. By 1941, many other ships did the same.

On December 27, 1941, the British performed a commando raid against the Germans off the Norwegian coast. The HMS Kenya cruiser, nicknamed *The Pink Lady*, only sustained minor damage - despite being fired on heavily by the Germans.

The only explanation was the paint of the ship blending in with the pink marker dye on the shells used by the Germans, making them unable to distinguish between the ship and their shell splashes.

Sadly, not many more experiments were performed with this shade with naval ships as leadership decided the pink made ships too visible during the daytime.

Across the sea, however, in the North African desert, a downed plane had rusted over time in the sands to a color that resembled...you guessed it...pink.

Called *Desert Pink*, this shade was used on a fleet of Series 2A Land Rovers, called *Pink Panthers*, throughout World War II in the desert. They were mainly used for operations behind-enemy-lines in the deserts of Oman, blending into the sands to become practically invisible.

Maybe this is why historical maps of Britain always showed the country in pink.

During this time, Nazi concentration camps forced suspected homosexuals to wear a pink triangle as identification. This is why the pink triangle has become a symbol of the modern gay rights movement.

Historians believe that the push for pink as a feminine color happened after World War II in an effort to reestablish traditional Western gender roles. Women had to go back to domestic roles, so advertisers pushed to "refeminize" them with ads of housewives in frilly, pink clothing.

Pink's popularity exploded in the United States in the presidential inauguration of Dwight D. Eisenhower in 1953, when his wife, Mamie, wore a pink dress to the inauguration. Women saw this as the epitome of fashion and being seen as "ladylike". The 1957 musical *Funny Face* cemented this as a feminine color, followed by public figures like Jacqueline Kennedy and Marilyn Monroe.

Magenta

We've talked about the industrial chemistry revolution, which occurred in the mid-nineteenth century, where many of the colors we've discussed developed their synthetic alternatives.

This started with pink shades, specifically *mauveine*, invented by William Perkin in 1856.

In 1858, France, François-Emmanuel Verguin mixed *aniline*

(a key component in *mauveine*) with *carbon tetrachloride*. This created a reddish-purple dye he named *fuchsine* after the flower.

At the same time, two British chemists, Chambers Nicolson and George Maule, did a similar experiment and named the resulting color *roseine*. They later changed the name to *magenta* in 1860. But why?

In 1859, during the *Second Italian War of Independence*, a huge battle was fought by France and Sardinia against the Austrians near the town of Magenta, Italy. Napoleon II's soldiers crossed the nearby river, outflanked the Austrian army and caused them to retreat. The Austrians, however, were trapped. Confined terrain made the fighting hand to hand as the French and Sardinians battled the Austrians. Rumor is the battlefield was so red from the blood that the *fuchsine/roseine* dye (discovered three years beforehand) was renamed magenta in tribute. The name lived on.

Magenta started to be used in paintings during this time, with works such as *Psyche*, by Bouguereau, *Portrait of Marie Lagadu*, by Paul Gauguin, and *Les toits de Colloure*, by Henri Matisse. In the 1960s, magenta became more associated with psychedelic art.

In 1860, a book came out, calling out magenta as an important innovation (*English Women's Clothing in the Nineteenth Century: A Comprehensive Guide*). It reports that the color was so admired it was called the 'Queen of Colours', used for dresses, petticoats, bonnets, stockings and ribbons.

In the 20th century, Italian designer Elsa Schiaparelli created a new pink chemical dye called *shocking pink*. She mixed magenta with white to get a brighter pink color. Her fashions and even her *Shocking* perfume featured this new pink color.

The color Magenta, named after a bloody battle, we've now

seen pushed to become associated with more bold statements. In 1984, a magenta top with the slogan "Rock Against Reagan" solidified the color with revolution. They were sold by a series of punk rock concerts dedicated to protest President Ronald Reagan.

Now, let's fast-forward to 2001 with the introduction of the wireless carrier, T-Mobile. They launched with a brand color that had never been associated with phones before - magenta.

Why on earth did they pick that color? I'm sure competitors like AT&T and Verizon laughed. What were they thinking? As I learned the power of the color, however, I dug into their stats.

In 2020, T-Mobile US had a revenue of approximately 68.4 billion U.S. dollars. They also overtook AT&T as America's #2 Wireless Provider. How does a company convince 250 million people - including 10% of Sprint's customer traffic - to move over to them?

They call themselves the un-carrier, to vividly emphasize that they are doing something radically different. Clearly, it worked.

T-Mobile uses magenta to symbolize radical difference. Going against the grain. Revolution.

BEHAVIOR

Pink

Do we really respond to the color pink physically?

I came across an experiment done in the 1970s by Alexander G. Schauss. He wanted to see how pink affected moods and behavior. After finding a shade that seemed to have the most calming reaction, he was able to convince the US Naval Correctional Center in Seattle to paint the walls and ceiling of an admission cell this pink - bartering naming the color after the two willing military officers in exchange if it worked. Fifteen minutes of *Baker-Miller Pink* exposure reduced aggression in the detainees for up to thirty minutes after leaving the room. Thirty minutes! (Hex code is #FF91AF)

"Even if a person tries to be angry or aggressive in the presence of pink, he can't," says Schauss. "The heart muscles can't race fast enough. It's a tranquilizing color that saps your energy."

This was proven by having subjects stare at a square of pink paper with their arms outstretched. Schauss would try to push their arms back down, which he could do easily when they stared at pink. When subjects stared at blue and did the same thing, Schauss could not force their arms down. (This practice is called muscle-testing.)

Adam Alter, Professor of Marketing and Psychology at NYU, reports adjustments in people's behavior in his bestseller, *Drunk Tank Pink*. He describes the *Baker-Miller Pink* sensation where people, utilizing Schauss' experiments, went on a pink-painting spree! Psychiatrists, dentists, doctors, teachers and even parents put this color on their walls. Bus companies reported decreased vandalism after painting their seats bright pink, as did housing estates with violent behavior.

But there was a problem. 30 years later, psychologist Oliver Genschow repeated experiments using *Baker-Miller Pink* and saw the opposite reaction in inmates...even increased aggression.

What could have caused this? Remember the "after effect" we talked about in the Green chapter when surgeons stared at red for too long? If someone is around pink too long, wouldn't our eyes categorize it to its primary color additive - which is red? It would be interesting to investigate to see if this is in fact what happens. That prisoners who are in a pink environment too long start having an "after effect" of seeing red. That would certainly explain the sudden change of behavior to aggression with what we've seen in red behavioral studies.

Enter Swiss psychologist Daniela Späth in 2011. She painted a new shade, called *Cool Down Pink*, (a lighter pink closer to #FACDE5) in 10 prisons across Switzerland. Her studies showed over the next four years that prisoners had less aggressive behavior and relaxed more quickly if they were in these pink cells.

If you look at *Baker-Miller Pink* and *Cool Down Pink*, there is actually quite a difference between them in color mixing. *Baker-Miller Pink* is much closer to red, highly saturated, with no gray mixed in. *Cool Down Pink*, however, is more desaturated with a bit of gray.

We know that pink weakens muscle strength and reduces heart rate. And you'll learn soon that gray mutes personalities. Is it any surprise that Späth's new shade had such a lasting effect? Absolutely not.

Now we know that pink is a powerful color when it comes to influencing behavior. That we can see it, wear it, paint it, design with it and it will affect someone when it's viewed. The color that does not exist in the visible light spectrum. Colors of all kinds hold power - even if they do not come from light frequency.

Magenta

Unlike pink, magenta has no behavioral experiments or studies I could find. Fortunately, I can share a pretty striking story from a client of mine.

Kay Brown, founder of Four 4 Consent, has a passion for ending nightlife violence in the electronic music industry. When they first came to me, it was apparent the company needed a color that said a lot with little to no words. We came up with magenta as they are leading a nightlife revolution and wanting to empower victims to stand up for themselves and music industry professionals to lead the charge for change.

"When changing our primary brand color from pink to magenta, we didn't expect much difference, but our agency was surprised by the response. We began to get more contacts that were interested in our organization and more reach outs outside of just music and nightlife. We have expanded into entertainment and gaming spaces throughout the last year by serving clients and helping with consulting and training. These colors not only resonated with our initial audience but helped pull in a closely related sector to help make these areas safer and support victims who have experienced harm." - Kay Brown, Four 4 Consent

It's been incredible to see the influence a simple color change has made for the company. Not only has their client list expanded, but they are continuously getting contacted for more press features and people are spreading the word.

CURRENT CULTURE & RELIGION

Pink

We have many common phrases using the word *pink*. "In the pink" - to be in good health. "Pink slip" - to be fired from a job.

"Pink-collar worker" - jobs thought of as women's work. "Tickled pink" - which means extremely pleased.

In 2008, *Breast Cancer Awareness Month* adopted the color pink as a symbol of empowerment for women fighting breast cancer. This has become associated with a pink ribbon.

In India, pink turbans are worn at Hindu weddings.

In France, the academic dress of Medicine and Health for graduates is redcurrant, a red shade of pink.

Since 1893, the *London Financial Times* newspaper has used salmon pink coloring for its newsprint. In England and Wales during legal proceedings, a brief delivered to a barrister is usually tied with a pink ribbon. It is the color associated with the defense.

In Spain and Italy, a romance novel is called a *pink novel*.

Pink is a symbol of joy and happiness, used for the Third Sunday of Advent and the Fourth Sunday of Lent in the Catholic Church.

Rose is the color associated with the heart chakra in Yogic Hindu, Shaktic Hindu and Tantric Buddhist beliefs. Pink is most associated with Meher Baba, an Indian spiritual leader who wore pink to please Mehera Irani, a female follower who loved the color.

Magenta

The Reserve Bank Of India released a magenta-colored banknote in 2016. It is the highest currency note printed that's currently in circulation.

In Indonesia, the Marine Corps have magenta colored beret's.

Aircraft autopilot systems usually display course paths in magenta.

The only countries with magenta in their flag are Cantabria

of Spain, Magenta of France and Cartago of Columbia as of 2022.

Pope Francis has been named "The Magenta Catholic" due to his more liberal Catholic leanings, desire for an inclusive, decentralized Church and focus on environmentalism.

In Northern India, the *Gulabi Gang* is a women's movement formed in 2006 aimed to reduce female oppression. They dress entirely in Magenta.

NATURE

Pink

Pink is seen beautifully in many gemstones and minerals throughout the world. *Pink topaz* in Brazil. *Corundum* from Tazmania. *Calcite* from Morocco. *Pink Sandstone* in Utah. *Barite-Rhodochrosite* from China. *Rose Quartz*. Even pink colored sand in the beaches of French Polynesia.

We also see plenty of pink in wildlife. The *Strigilla carnaria's* shell, *Ocelated frogfish, pink iguana, pink dolphin, white elephant,* pink *pig, Roseate spoonbill, Lophochroa leadbeateri,* and pink *flamingo* (although the flamingo's coloring is based entirely by diet).

Lake Hillier in Australia is even pink due to its algae!

Pink is also one of the most common flower colors. We can see this with the pink *rose,* the *clematis Chantilly,* pink *hibiscus,* pink *tulips,* pink *dahlia,* pink *peony,* blooms of the *Japanese cherry tree* and many, many more.

Magenta

Magenta/fuchsia can be seen in the *Fuchsia* plant, the original inspiration for the dye color. It can also be seen in the *Orchid Phalaenopsis, Rhododendron, Clematis* "Sunset", *Geranium sanguineum, Dahlia* "Hillcrest Royal", Rambler *rose* and *cactus* flower.

Coral from the Persian Gulf showcases the color, as does the *Anisoptera Ana Cotta* "dragonfly" and the *Pseudanthias tuka* reef fish.

HEALING

Pink

The color pink, according to Noah Goldhirsh, "encourages conversation, peace, sharing an understanding, helping us to open our hearts to love". She uses pink therapy to help clients release emotional distress and share their true feelings.

Magenta/Fuschia

Magenta is a color that can be used in light healing, according to Charles Klotsche. In color medicine, magenta can balance the emotions, level blood pressure and stimulate the kidneys, adrenals and heart. He has found the color magenta to vibrate at 621 trillion times per second.

As this is our last section on healing, I'd like to share with you a quote from Klotsche to help you further understand this concept of light as a healing power.

"Our twelve vibrating colors generate electrical impulses and magnetic currents or fields of energy that are prime activators of the biochemical and hormonal process in the human body, the stimulants or sedatives necessary to balance the entire system and its organs." - Charles Klotsche, *Color Medicine*

MUSIC

I was unable to find any relation of pink or magenta to a frequency of light as a wavelength of vibration. Klotsche did find a vibration for magenta, so this needs further study.

FILM

Film and television have used pink for decades to symbolize the obliteration of innocence. There are many, many films where pink is associated with variances of evil.

Vanity with 'The Plastics' in *Mean Girls* and corruption with 'The Pink Ladies' in *Grease*. Plastic, fake personas in *Gentlemen Prefer Blondes, What A Way To Go* and *Legally Blonde*. Even false safety and support in *Harry Potter* with the character of Dolores Umbridge, who in fact hates children.

Looking at the beloved movie, *Dumbo*, both pink and magenta are used. Pink on the mother's cap, Dumbo's ears and even his face paint to portray innocence. But when he accidentally gets drunk and a hallucinogenic scene ensues, the scary elephant hallucinations are magenta.

Now we have to move into the main genre pink and magenta are used in: horror.

Carrie and her iconic prom dress. *Suspiria. Pretty In Pink. It Follows. Jennifer's Body. Cam.* Over and over, even in children's television (*My Little Pony, Power Rangers, Miraculous Ladybug*) or films (*Aladdin, Alice In Wonderland, Princess and the Frog*), pink and magenta mean evil.

WHY YOU LOVE IT

Pink

If you love pink, you are both a comforting creature and a creature of comfort. People who love pink are usually softer, more feminine and loving. They form comfortable connections, but usually not too deep. Focusing on the lighter side of life, pink lovers want to keep things pleasant, warm and soft.

Although confrontations and deep matters can make you uncomfortable, pink is your retreat and very reflective in your environment: home, office, clothing and even makeup, hair or nails.

Magenta

If magenta is a color you love, you are a spitfire of a human. Usually a more bold, assertive personality, you have views and are absolutely unafraid to voice them...possibly to the extreme. You align yourself to people who share your views and push them publicly whenever possible.

You may be strongly for the feminist movement, political change or gay rights.

Although it can be isolating, you express yourself adamantly with this color as your visual voice and know you can make a difference in this world with your beliefs.

WHY YOU HATE IT

Pink

People usually hate pink for one of two reasons. Being seen as too feminine by a parent or peers, or trauma from watching films as a child.

If you hate pink, you may be very resistant to the sensitive nature of your being. You probably bottle your emotions and are absolutely awful at sharing your feelings.

You tie the feminine and sensitive to negativity and avoid it at all costs, choosing much stronger, more masculine colors to create a hardened shell around the softer side of yourself.

Magenta

If you hate magenta, it may be tied to culture. Usually, as the color is so closely associated with revolutions and political beliefs of one kind or another, your dislike of the color solidified after an experience.

Maybe you saw the "Rock Against Regan" movement, pushy advertising by T-Mobile, the genitalia-themed hats after President Trump's first election in women's marches, or even the magenta themed attire by political leaders during the pro-abortion movement of 2022.

Any of these experiences, or others, could have muddied your interest and appreciation for the color based on personal bias.

What's so hard to remember is that colors are manipulated by people, not the other way around.

IMPLEMENTING IT INTO YOUR LIFE

Pink

This is the perfect color to use to bring more softness into your life. To smooth rough edges of your personal communication and to bring down your heart rate in a calming, supportive way.

Maybe tensions are running high in your household and you've decided pink would be a good color to bring into your living space. A rug, piece of furniture or artwork could be a subtle change that has a major impact. Or you want to bring more ease to a tense relationship. This would be a good color to wear when you're around them to disarm.

Magenta

Magenta is a great color to use sparingly and to support the aspects of your life where you need to step forward. Maybe you want a promotion, or to join a local charity, but just haven't taken the leap...magenta can help you get there.

Just remember, magenta can definitely jar the senses, so use it in pops when you have a specific intention you want to support.

I was definitely humbled by studying pink and magenta. Two colors I had previously disregarded, as they were not in the visible light spectrum, are both incredibly and intimately related to human behavior and our environment.

It blows me away a color that our brains technically make up define so much of our history and responses. These are colors we can no longer ignore.

As we've learned, these two colors thought by many to be in the same color family, could not have more different meanings. That's why I dedicated time in this chapter to separating the two so we could learn as much as possible in order to more clearly communicate.

Can you imagine wearing pink to a competition where you need to really increase your heart rate? Oops.

Or magenta to a conflict resolution meeting? Double oops.

Now you understand the difference. And now you can make impactful decisions with either color in your day to day life - whether you're going to battle with magenta, or painting that entryway pink to calm those kids down!

Magenta and pink are the only two non-spectral colors I firmly believe are a part of our universal color language. Now we are well on our way to speaking this language fluently.

SECTION THREE

INJECTING COLOR LANGUAGE INTO YOUR LIFE

WHAT THE COLORS IN YOUR CLOSET SAY ABOUT YOU

Even if we aren't aware of it as children, we marvel at the world of color.

We want bright pink, blue or purple in our clothing and our toys. Bright movies make us light up - we want to watch them over and over again.

And yet, somewhere along the way, the awe disappears.

Life sets in. Or should I say "reality"...becoming a grown up with a real job in the real world. Somehow grown-up-ness tells us to dull our senses, our expectations, even our wardrobe.

Think that you're different?

I want you to walk to your closet right now. What do you see?

Most people would see a litany of blacks, grays and whites with some blue jeans. You may be a bit more adventurous with a blue top or a yellow dress. But for the most part? Closets are usually - and unfortunately - monochromatic.

I remember making this discovery in college. We were supposed to do some sort of themed dress up day and yet here

I was, staring at my closet that looked more like a vampire's than a nineteen year old's.

What had happened? Why was it all so...colorless?

Here's what I think causes a lack of color in our closets: hurts, illnesses, traumas and wounds...

It's easy for me to say - after years of physical recovery from illness - that my past had ripped the desire for color right out of my life. Because with every setback, a part of my body shut down. And since nothing on earth affects the body's responses more than color, the best way to keep everything shut down was to wear colors that sparked no physical reaction whatsoever.

This wasn't intentional, of course. It was instinctual. My mind was protecting me from feeling. At the same time, however, my mind was preventing me from healing. The same may be true for you if your current closet is vampiresque as well.

I find this to be the case with most clients I see. They wear a lot of black. And even though they start very defensive, saying it's always been 'their color', the wheels quickly start turning in their minds. Almost instantaneously, they start sending me photos of colorful shirts, flowers or wall paint they see as they continue through their day after our consult. Then they start experimenting with pops of color - usually on their skin.

Every single time, the people close to them react to the change. Their kids get a huge surge of energy, which inspires the parent to take them on an adventure or road trip to continue the joy. Their customers suddenly start pounding down their door. Even their mood starts to shift in a new and unexpected way; where their mind clears and they focus in on what they've always wanted to do in their career or vacation time.

Nine times out of ten, they tell me that color has helped them tap in to who they really are. That it opens up a new door.

My goal here is to show you how multifaceted color can be and how you can harness its power into a language with your body, your closet, your marketing...even your brunch dates with mom.

Let's talk about the monochromatic nightmare that can be *gray,* or *grey,* depending on where you live in the world.

I know what you're thinking.

"My walls are gray! It's my favorite color inside!"

Mine are too, friend. But I do make sure the undertones are blue or yellow. By now, you should know why. If not, go back and read those color chapters.

Gray has been used for many years on streets, buildings and especially - you guessed it - jails. Only in the 2000's have we really started using the color inside of our homes. And, although it can be very beautiful, we have to fully understand the power of gray in order to use it in a way that doesn't damage our personality over time.

Let me explain.

Gray does not exist in the visible light spectrum. That means that it is not a color that comes from the sun. It's not a part of the rainbow. Agreed? We've already established the seven spectral colors (*red, orange, yellow, green, blue, indigo, violet*). We combined indigo and blue into *'blue'* as they create similar reactions in the body and behavior. And we call violet *'purple'* for the same reason. The only other two colors that are non-spectral that cause a reaction in the body are *magenta* and *pink.*

Here are the final 8 colors of color communication:

- Red
- Orange
- Yellow
- Green
- Blue
- Purple
- Pink
- Magenta

Colors like black, brown and gray do not affect the body in the same way. At least not positively. Gray, for example, is known to mute personalities over time.

Let me give you an example. On Netflix, there was a show called *The Circle*. A group of random people are chosen to live in apartments all in one building for the duration of the competition. The only interaction they have with each other is via *The Circle,* which is a social platform that links them together via on-screen app. No voice, no face, just text. Each contestant gets their own apartment and each one has a totally different design scheme. Now let's talk about my favorite contestant, Joey. Yes, you can absolutely picture Joey from *Friends* here - I'm sure they could have been cousins. He loves family, lasagna, has immense home-town pride and wants to work out all of the time.

Now, Joey's apartment was filled with gray walls. The other contestants were not. Not a big deal to anyone watching I'm sure, but to me, I was worried. I knew gray over time would heavily subdue his personality. He would become more monotone, less enthusiastic and mellow out noticeably. It took a few days but sure enough, I started noticing a difference. A few days after that, my husband noticed without me saying anything.

Thank goodness he still went on to win the first season - but it made me wonder if the set designers did that purposefully. If not, they better pick up this book so they don't accidentally influence a contestant's personality next season!

Gray isn't all bad, mind you.

I'm sure after reading about Joey, you can understand why prisons are painted gray: to mute emotions and personalities. There are even cases where school uniforms are made gray for this purpose - to keep students more muted so there's less conflict.

If you are having chronic anxiety or stress, it may be helpful to wear the color occasionally until the event passes. Then switch to a more healing color to gradually support you, easing the ongoing issue. For example, if I need to focus and complete a work assignment that takes up a lot of brain energy, I usually wear gray. I don't want anything to be overly stimulated, so the color supports me with that intention for a limited amount of time.

If your closet is full of grays, browns, blacks and whites, there is nothing for your body to react to. And if you don't spend any time in the sun, you are not giving yourself the colors needed for your body to achieve peak function since hormones run our bodies according to light. Your body is ultimately starving for light.

A slow incorporation of all of the primary communication colors in your wardrobe is a great place to start in your color journey. Not only will this start waking up your reactions, but it will help you communicate more effectively in your daily life. For example, you may wear red to a toastmasters meeting tomorrow to help empower your speech. Or purple to a lunch date to communicate your openness for a new relationship.

For now, however, I want you to take a drive into your nearby city and look around. How much gray do you see? Can you understand why it's used? Do you think color would change things if it was introduced?

Here in Coeur D'Alene, Idaho, people paint transformer boxes.

A gray box in the middle of the street doesn't seem like a big deal. But if you count them on your way to the store, you'll easily rack up a dozen. So why not bring some color?

My drive to Pilgrim's local market is now full of naturescapes, eagles, fish, sunflowers and blue sky. A tiny change with a big impact. What tiny change can you make today that will have a big impact?

Moving forward, I want to give you a "cheat sheet" when it comes to using color in your wardrobe. That way, for the next few weeks, you can open to this page when you're getting ready in the morning to support your day's intention.

Color Closet Cheat Sheet

- **Red:** Power and attention-grabbing. Wear if you are leading something: a meeting, a class, a team or if you are public speaking to get someone's attention. Keep in mind it will increase you and your audience's blood pressure, heart rate and fight or flight reflex.
- **Orange:** Balance and family-attracting. Wear if you want to feel more balanced when going about your day or if you are trying to bring people together in a harmonious way. Remember that orange is also a stimulating color, so if you need to cool down a

situation, you may want to switch to purple instead.

- **Yellow:** Focus and joy. Wear if you want to bring life to your day, inspire happiness around you and create more focus in your activities. Avoid if you are those close to you deal with anxiety, fearfulness or hypersensitivity. Stick to cooler tones in this case.

- **Green:** Growth and self-identity. Wear if you want to speak in your truest voice today and bring calm to your environment. This color will cause people to open up to you and see you as the grounding force. Be cautious with shades as we know this can be seen as the 'split personality color', so avoid if you'll be in a situation today where someone chooses between you and another candidate as this color may make them second guess things.

- **Blue:** Trust and inspiration. Wear if you want to bring more trust and intellectual thoughts to your day. Others will be naturally attracted to this as its such a world-favorite color. But do not use if you want people out of their heads for certain decisions or interactions. This is the color of the mind!

- **Purple:** Relationships and spirituality. Wear if you want to bring more expression and connection into your day. This will make people tune into their spiritual side and connect more deeply with you. Avoid in environments where the spiritual and mystic may be frowned upon or judged.

- **Pink:** Comfort and innocence. Wear if you want a soft, comfortable day. This color will help soothe interactions today and give you a peaceful outlook on things. Do not use if you absolutely do no want to be perceived as feminine or possibly naive.

- **Magenta:** Revolution and attention-grabbing.
  Wear if you want to make a statement and make
  people notice you. Please wear responsibly as we've
  already discussed the negative connotations built
  around this color from how people have worn it.
  Magenta will support your movement, so be kind to
  this powerful color in your decision making.

Go forth and wear color! And tag us on social media so we can
see you living your life with more color in your wardrobe.

EATING COLOR

"To live in color:

From the colour our representation spread out in organism.

From the representation of colour, feelings.

From the felt and represented colour, impulse."

-Rudolph Steiner, Goethe scholar, 1921

As WE ALL come to grasp with the fact that color can very much guide our feelings and therefore our actions, there is a very simple way of incorporating this process into our daily lives. Food!

You may start with wearing a color, painting a room, getting out in nature, but food is something we ingest every single day. Since our body uses this for fuel, which leads to cellular replenishment, why not use what we know about light colors to aid this process?

Below, you'll find a list of foods in each visible light spectrum color that you can use when making choices for your meals. Phytochemist Lisa Ganora provides wonderful explanations of what happens on a molecular level when we ingest specific colors in her book *Herbal Constituents: Foundations of Phytochemistry.*

I also recommend researching the nutrition factors for each food so you can fully understand the benefits to your body function.

Red

Inside of red foods, you will find *xanthophylls* and *anthocyanins.* Two *xanthophylls* called *capsanthin* and *capsorubin* are in spicy reds like red peppers and chili peppers. Theses are powerful and long-lasting antioxidants that protect cell membranes.

- Apples
- Cranberries
- Red beets
- Red cabbage
- Red tomatoes
- Red bell peppers
- Radishes
- Red chili pepper
- Cayenne
- Radicchio
- Red leaf lettuce
- Rhubarb
- Red onion
- Red potatoes
- Red grapes
- Pomegranate
- Strawberries

- Watermelon
- Raspberries
- Red cherries
- Red plum
- Blood oranges
- Goji berry
- Kidney beans
- Muntingia
- Paprika
- Redcurrant
- Red rice
- Sumac

Orange

Orange (and yellow) foods contain *cartenoids*, which protect our cell membranes - keeping our blood lipids from being damaged from oxidation or free radical damage. These foods also contain *curcumin*, a supreme antioxidant and anti-inflammatory.

- Orange carrots
- Pumpkin
- Butternut squash
- Oranges
- Sweet potato
- Grapefruit
- Mamey sapote
- Atomic orange corn
- Peaches
- Mango

- Papaya
- Maprang
- Tangerine
- Pomelo
- Kumquat
- Cantelope
- Red lentils
- Chanterelle mushroom
- Chicken of the woods
- Orange cauliflower
- Orange swiss chard
- Clementine
- Dalandan
- Gac
- Kabocha squash
- Kaho watermelon
- Mila orange pear tomato
- Orange accordian tomato
- Orange bell pepper
- Orange habanero
- Persimmon
- Salmonberry
- Tamarillo

Yellow

See orange explanation above, as yellow foods cause the same effect in the cells.

- Yellow squash
- Lemons

- Yellow pepper
- Yellow tomatoes
- Yellow apples
- Apricots
- Pineapple
- Banana
- Yellow corn
- Saffron
- Yellow chard
- Semolina
- Olive oil
- Turmeric
- Star fruit
- Acorn squash
- Yellow fig
- Golden kiwi
- Yellow chili
- Yellow cherry
- Mirabelle plum
- Eggfruit
- Jackfruit
- Yellow dragon fruit
- Durian
- Summer squash
- Yellow watermelon

Green

Green foods give our body *chlorophyll, folic acid* and and *folate*. Our hemoglobin structure is almost identical to chlorophyll molecules. Chlorophyll also helps us produce sugar and glucose. Folic acid develops the nervous system and builds the blood.

- Cucumber
- Zucchini
- Green grapes
- Pear
- Broccoli
- Spinach
- Cabbage
- Lettuce
- Brussels sprouts
- Green beans
- Peas
- Green pepper
- Green apples
- Kiwi
- Lime
- Avocado
- Asparagus
- Parsley
- Thyme
- Dill
- Oregano
- Zatar
- Nopal
- Edamame
- Collard greens
- Spinach
- Basil
- Seaweed
- Mung beans
- Arugula

- Mustard greens
- Celery
- Artichoke
- Bitter gourd
- Leek
- Mint
- Okra
- Watercress
- Cactus

Blue

- There are no true blue foods

Purple

Purple foods contain *anthocyanins*, which are antioxidants, anti-inflammatories and cancer-preventative molecules.

- Blueberries
- Eggplant
- Purple cabbage
- Purple potatoes
- Blackberries
- Purple grapes
- Plums
- Figs
- Acai berry
- Fiesole artichokes

- Black currant
- Forbidden rice
- Purple mangosteen
- Purple asparagus
- Purple basil
- Purple broccoli
- Purple carrots
- Redbor kale
- Purple vienna kohlrabi
- Purple yam
- Purple star apple
- Elderberries
- Red dragon fruit
- Purple barley
- Bilberries
- Chokeberries
- Belgian endive
- Purple pod pole greens
- Purple corn
- Purple garlic

As you cook with these colorful foods, know that you are not only nourishing your body but giving your brain stimulation, improving your mental processes and sparking creativity.

If you would like to celebrate your colorful cooking with the color community, be sure to share your dishes on social media with us so we can inspire the world!

THE LIGHTS IN YOUR HOME
HELPFUL OR HURTFUL?

THE MOST CHALLENGING thing to understand when shifting your understanding of color is...how do we relate to it, exactly?

So many of us work late into the night or within a cubicle that we can't see color having that much of a transformational effect in our day to day life.

I thought it would be helpful to break down for you exactly what light we're seeing when outdoors and indoors - and how color is involved in both.

Let's start with natural light from the sun.

The visible light spectrum, as a reminder, ranges in frequencies from about 380 nanometers to 780 nanometers. Less than 380 puts us into ultraviolet rays (that certain animals like bees and chickens can see), x-rays and gamma rays. Over 780 is the territory of infrared rays, radar, FM and AM waves.

If we're looking at the breakdown of exact frequencies in nanometers, here are where the colors fall:

- Violet: 395-430

- Indigo: 430-450
- Blue: 450-480
- Blue/Green: 480-520
- Green: 520-555
- Yellow/Green: 555-585
- Yellow: 585-600
- Amber: 600-615
- Orange: 615-625
- Orange/Red: 625-640
- Red: 640-700

This means that everything that grows on earth - including humans, plants and animals - absorb light frequencies between 380 to 780 nanometers to make our hormones or chlorophyll.

With me so far?

Now let's look at artificial light.

For those of us gardeners who live in challenging climates, we may want to extend our growing season. This would require using artificial light to keep plants growing without sunlight.

Those lights would need to range from 610-700 nanometers for optimal growth, since that's the main frequency of light they need. This is well within the visible light spectrum of frequencies and resonates between amber, orange and red light.

LED lights, which we all use now in our homes, schools, offices and public buildings, are all commonly at 400 nanometers. From the chart, we see that 400 nanometers is barely in the visible light spectrum of violet and is very closet to ultraviolet light.

This is extremely interesting, since there are many warnings saying to NEVER look directly into an LED bulb as it can damage the eyes.

So, what are LED lights really made of? The answer is ultraviolet light, ranging from:

- UV-C: 100-280
- UV-B: 280-320
- UV-A: 320-396

We do have these spectrum's of light from the sun naturally. UV-B light is known to cause sunburns and UV-C is known to actually kill life. Fortunately, the ozone layer filters out all contact with UV-C light from the sun and a certain amount of UV-B.

UV-A is the main ultraviolet light emitted from LED bulbs, but it does contain amounts of UV-B and UV-C. UV-A light is the least harmful (this is the only UV light the human eye can partially see) but it can possibly lead to skin aging, damage and some institutions say skin cancer.

In 2016, the American Medical Association stated that life-long exposure of the retina and lens to blue peaks from LEDs can increase the risk of cataract and age-related macular degeneration. This is intrinsically linked to LEDs resonating in the blue end of the light spectrum, along with overall exposure to ultraviolet light.

You're probably wondering what you can use instead of an LED light. From my research, you can use a full-spectrum bulb. This is created to mimic the full spectrum of light, similar to the sun. This is not the same as a daylight bulb. There is some-thing called a *Color Rendering Index*, or CRI, which measures how accurately light renders the colors of the objects it's bouncing off of (compared to how real sunlight would). LED's range score as low as 60%. Most daylight bulbs have a CRI of around 80%. Full-spectrum lights can have as high as 96% or even 100%.

We can easily see that plants can only grow if they have access to light ranging from 610-700 nanometers. LEDs range from 100-400, so we need access to an artificial light source that contains the full spectrum of visible light.

You can choose your grow lights with this knowledge, making sure they contain a larger spectrum of light. And you can get a light at your desk that mimics sunlight to more positively effect your mood. But, as human beings, we do need true sunlight daily for optimum function. There is no 100% artificial replacement.

Humans, plants and animals are dependent on light from the sun to create and balance our hormone production, which means that color is crucial to our existence.

Artificial light can have some definite health benefits when used correctly and encompassing the visible light spectrum frequencies, but exposure to LED's on a consistent basis in our environment is a recipe for eventual imbalance in our bodies.

COLOR ADVERTISING
ARE YOU ALREADY BEING MANIPULATED?

ONE OF THE most painful things to observe is how certain industries know this information about color psychology and abuse it by using colors to manipulate a buyer when it may not be in their best interest.

As I've stated, color does not manipulate - people do.

One of my biggest goals is to show people color language so they can use it for positive communication and change. More importantly, however, I want people to feel empowered to recognizing when it's being used against them in manipulative ways.

Let me paint the positive goal here.

You can use color in your business to attract the right customer who would benefit from your services. After doing an intensive study into your ideal client's emotions, needs and struggles, you can choose the best primary brand color to attract them. Knowing the pain point you help resolve, you can ease their customer journey by signaling what you do with visual color cues.

For example, a family therapist can pick the color purple,

signaling to target customers that they want to support the growth of families and relationships. Because, in truth, that's what this business owner does and how they truly help someone.

This is the goal of businesses using color...or at least it should be.

What we have to stop is the outright manipulation and fear-based marketing that is being done in public arenas today through politics, toys, foods and pharmaceuticals.

Why do you think the United States has tied the top political parties, democrats and republicans, to blue and red? From this book, you know they are both psychological primaries that hit the body and the mind. Do you really think that's accidental?

Watch the news. Observe how much red and blue you see - no matter the news channel. The ones that are aware of this (which are all of the national ones) will add these color schemes to manipulate the viewer to get angry or afraid. And yes, those are the only two options.

I'll show you in the next chapter how even a tie color can influence an election.

Next, start watching toy commercials and pay attention at your local store. What colors are being used? Studies date back to the mid 1950's of psychologists readily admitting they use color to manipulate the desires of children.

Are we really okay with that? Is it truly for their best benefit?

From the pigment and dye history we've read in this book, we know the dangers most dyes carry, even in their synthetic form. Do you feel informed whenever you go to a toy store of what exactly is in toys in terms of materials used?

We need to spend time researching before making buying decisions. There are many eco-friendly toy companies that do not use toxic dyes or led; Finn + Emma, Hape, Holtztiger, Camden Rose, Uncle Goose, or PlanToys, for example.

Now let's transition into food advertising. What colors are being used at restaurants?

I remember when Taco Bell changed their branding a few years ago to a very distinct purple. Very unusual for a to-go food chain. I wondered why. You've read the purple chapter, so you should be wondering the same thing. Why would a fast-food chain want to start being associated with the spiritual and non-corporeal?

Taco Bell's Super Bowl Ad in 2022 answered the question, where Doja Cat had become the new spokesperson. A much more eccentric performer, this also paired with Taco Bell's new messaging, including words like "magic trick", "witchcraft" and "sorcery" (you can read this for yourself on their website and menu descriptions).

Food companies' branding is something to stay consistently aware of. They already manipulate us into feeling more hungry using colors like red, yellow and orange.

Let's look at McDonalds. They are considered by most to be good fast food that can be eaten regularly. A recent commercial (2022) shows a father waking his sleeping son by waving a McDonalds bag in front of his nose. It's even called the 'Now I'm a Morning Person Deal'.

They were the first fast food restaurant to put one billion into their advertising. No one can tell me they would have taken that risk without knowing they'd make back their investment...and as of 2022, they are the second highest ranked restaurant brand in the world, right behind Starbucks. I didn't say fast-food brand. I said restaurant brand.

Pharmaceutical companies are the most skilled at manipulation with color psychology. Watch any commercial for a medication and you'll notice one very apparent primary color.

They put it everywhere: backgrounds, clothing, flowers and foods. The commercial will saturate you with their color palette. Because they know it makes the product sell.

You may be drawn to a specific medication that comes with five pages of warnings, but you're so drawn to the color used in a recent commercial, you'll instinctively choose it without being fully informed.

Obviously, each of these companies lists ingredients and side effects on their materials, so technically, what they do is 100% legal.

As I've stated, there's nothing wrong with advertising and using colors strategically to support your message. It's how we can communicate subconsciously to a buyer that we are the right helper for them to achieve their goals.

My issue is when it's used to force someone's instincts into a buying decision because a brand has figured out how to manipulate them. And that's what I've found predominantly happens with these four industries.

You can see how color language can be extremely manipulative and how important it is to have a strict morality code when it's being used.

However, there are currently no regulations for this because people do not see color as a language. Yet. My hope is that we can change this together so there is more integrity to color advertising.

You can explore more resources on the ethical use of color in branding, marketing and advertising at colorinstitute.com.

WHY RED & BLUE TIES
WIN PRESIDENCIES

HAVE you ever watched a political debate? I remember watching the final six Republican candidates on February 13, 2016. If you don't remember it, re-watch it when you finish this chapter. It's worth it to have your eyes opened to color in the political arena.

Here we are in a sea of red and blue: on the stage, on the speakers, even the lights on the audience.

Have you ever wondered why?

I don't have a history in politics, my history is in television and film. In the film industry, so much focus and attention is on celebrities at large events like the Oscars. Their outfit is probably the biggest focus, and the largest stress of that is the color. What color will the dress be? What color tie? Designers fight to be chosen - and they have to think of the best color and tone of color for that celebrity.

Is it any wonder that equal if not more importance would be placed on a politician?

In 2020, Nancy Pelosi and the *Democratic Women's Caucus*

all wore white to pledge solidarity to women's equality at the State of the Union address.

At Joe Biden's inauguration, many prominent leaders like Michelle Obama, Vice President Kamala Harris and First Lady Jill Biden all wore purple to symbolize unity. They did this because the combination of red and blue is...you guessed it... purple.

Politicians communicate with color because they - or their stylists - know exactly how to do so based on target market research.

Let's go back to the *Republican Presidential Candidate Debate* on February 13th, 2016.

Behind each candidate is a wall of a bright, vibrant red. Little flecks of blue shine above the wall. The candidates are mainly in black and gray suits. The only differentiator among each of them is their tie. The smallest piece of clothing visible.

Would it really make that much of an impact? Let's observe.

Half are wearing blue ties and half are wearing red.

In 1942, Russian scientist SV Krakov established through color experiments that red and blue had massive impacts on the body. People who saw red immediately increased their heart rate, blood pressure and pupil dilation. Blue had opposite results: reduced heart rate, blood pressure and no dilation of pupils.

With only these facts in mind, can we come to some quick conclusions about tie color choice?

We know blue ties would elicit a calming reaction and red would amp people up.

If you're trying to get a vote to be in the running for President, what response would you be looking for? For me, I'd want to pump people up and amplify their emotions. I'd also want to look strong regarding important Presidential topics such as leadership, military and security. Especially if I was trying to secure the Republican nomination.

Now let's look at the environment. Blue is historically associated with the democratic party, red with the republican party. It makes more sense in this environment running for President as a republican to wear a red tie.

That rules out Jeb Bush and John Kasich. Now we're down to four candidates.

Each of them are wearing red ties, so let's look at their shirt colors.

Ted Cruz is wearing a blue shirt. Donald Trump a white shirt. Ben Carson a white shirt. Marco Rubio a blue shirt.

Cruz and Rubio's blue shirts are completely neutralizing the red, which I would guess would cancel any effect whatsoever. To me, assessing just based on colors alone (not on personality, likes, dislikes or leanings), I would say the most votes would go to either Donald Trump or Ben Carson.

Now let's analyze the ties themselves. Ben Carson is in more of a soft red with florals and white dots. Donald Trump's is a bright, bright red. I don't think you could find a brighter red hex code.

Based on only the facts that I know about color, I told my family that night that Donald Trump would be the Republican candidate for President. They thought I was nuts.

Flash forward to February 25, 2016. It's the final *Republican Presidential Candidate Debate* between Donald Trump and Ted Cruz. Now Cruz is in the red tie and Trump in the blue.

Remember to look at the environment. What happened between the last debate and this one?

First of all, the tabloids, politicians and all of our friends were going crazy about Trump. Calling him names, airing dirty laundry...basically losing their minds. No one knew what to think about him, they just knew he was a hothead in front of the microphone who they were pretty sure they could not trust.

Let's now discuss the psychological primary influence of red and blue as a refresher. Red is physical, blue is mental. Red will make us react. It triggers a fight or flight response in our bodies. We are ready to physically respond to any threat. Blue, however, affects our intellect. It will make us think, mull things over and most importantly - trust.

In the previous debate, we were in the firestorm of the final six, where it's vital to stand out, be seen and convince people who is a powerful contender.

Now, we're in the final two. The goal to be seen has been achieved, so now the goal is to get the public to trust. Would you have changed your tie color too?

After this debate, I told my family: "Trump will win."

Still don't believe me? It's okay, they didn't either. Let's go one more round.

The date is September 26, 2016 and republican Donald Trump is going against democrat Hillary Clinton in the *Presidential Debate*. The backdrop behind them is completely blue.

Remember, you have to take your emotions out of this. We are only going by visuals, right?

Hillary is in head to toe fire engine red. Trump is in a bright, dark blue tie.

"He just won the presidency." Why? Because controversy swirled around both candidates in this final debate - one wore red and one wore blue. Trump convinced America to trust him subconsciously with a blue tie.

Flash forward to Thursday, October 22, 2020, where we see Donald Trump face off in the final *Presidential Debate* against Joe Biden. The backdrop, again, is entirely blue.

If you look at the footage, the candidates are dressed identically. Black suit, white shirt, United States of America flag pin, even the same shininess of their ties. The only difference?

Trump is in a red tie. Biden is in blue.

Even more controversy swirls around both candidates leading up to this debate. So why did Biden win?

He wore a blue tie and got us to trust him.

I was able to observe how each political party manipulated color in their campaign and I called two elections with my best guess based on color psychology. And, more importantly, now you may be able to as well.

If you're interested in learning more about the cultural use of color psychology for travel or international communication, get our Cultural Color Codes at colorinstitute.com.

CONCLUSION

93% of all communication is non-verbal.

We can deduce from that statistic that, no matter what language you speak, up to 90% of your meaning is not coming across (even if you are the most eloquent person in the world).

People are interpreting what, then? Sound to a certain extent, of course. Intonation, cadence, tone...but what about the rest? It would have to be visual. What people see.

After all of these chapters we've been through together, we know what the visual consists of. Light, which in our interpretation as human beings, is color.

Color is the only universal medium we all communicate with.

Proving undeniably that the only universal language, more powerful than any other spoken language, is color.

So, how do we speak it?

To a very high extent, we already are subconsciously. The beauty is that you now know the history, behavior, science, nature and interpretation of the eight colors of color language (red, orange, yellow, green, blue/indigo, purple/violet, pink, magenta). This means you will be able to purposefully use them when you communicate from here forward.

When you wake up, you'll be able to intentionally choose which color will assist your day's intention with your clothing.

You'll be able to choose what you eat not just based on caloric goals, but which colors will support different intentions in your body.

The colors of your home will change depending on the desire for each room for yourself, your partner and your family.

Your office space will change depending on what color you can support yourself with to effectively complete your work day and excel.

How you interact with others will change. You'll notice their 'color personality' immediately and understand how to balance it in your communication. For example, for an intellectually-driven person, you'll think *blue* and know to gear the conversation more cerebrally. An *orange* will be a totally different approach as your communication will be pointed towards balance.

Color is the compass that will point your communicative direction.

This beautiful language will touch every aspect of your life and how you communicate from this day forward. In fact, we know your brain has absorbed this book physically with expanded grey matter and is already putting it to use!

What a powerful arsenal you have in your pocket to support your life in every aspect!

Before you go, I'd love for you to take a moment with me. Let's make some observations.

- How do you feel about color now versus when you first started this book?

- Are you feeling any degree of awe or wonder now that you understand the many aspects of color?
- Have you instinctively started planning color injections into your wardrobe, home or office?
- Will you make more frequent trips into nature?

Color doesn't need an advocate, really. I know I've given you many pages of information, but that's all it is. Information.

Color, once noticed, speaks for itself. It moves thoughts and feelings without needing any support or encouragement. That is its innate nature, its own language.

The greatest gift for me is knowing I've simply made you aware of it. Color will take care of the rest.

I can't wait to see what happens now. Now that you have the tools of color communication and can truly speak this language fluently.

Welcome to the Universal Language Of Color™.

CONNECT WITH COLOR

As we move forward with this life-changing concept, I would like to invite you to join our color revolution at The Color Institute™.

There are plenty of resources for you to enjoy, whether you are decorating your home, re-strategizing your closet, branding/marketing your business or focusing on your health. We hold the only Universal Color Psychology Standard™-based curriculum.

- Courses
- Workshops
- Certifications
- Templates
- PDFs
- Consults

Visit us at www.colorinstitute.com or on social media @colorpsychologist.

Want to send a copy of this book to a friend or colleague? Or make our day with a review of your favorite stand outs? Please go to colorinstitute.com or email us at hello@colorinstitute.com.

ABOUT THE AUTHOR

Michelle Lewis is a globally recognized expert in color psychology; bridging the gap between science, education and real-world impact. Featured in TEDx, Clinical Advisor, Business Insider, The New York Post, Inc. and more – Michelle is known for translating the universal language of color into real-world applications. Her book, **Color Secrets: Learning the One Universal Language We Were Never Taught,** has become a cornerstone for understanding how color history shapes decisions, emotions and outcomes.

She is the founder of the **Universal Color Psychology Standard™** – the only universal standard showing how to correctly understand, interpret and implement color psychology across all industries. She also coined the phrase the Universal Language of Color™.

Michelle's expertise has driven measurable success for businesses & empowered academic institutions to **prepare the next generation of industry leaders**. With a unique ability to captivate and educate, Michelle is the trusted partner for CEO's, educators and creatives seeking to understand the transformative power of color.

You can see her work at colorinstitute.com.

BIBLIOGRAPHY

COLOR & THE BRAIN

- American Optometric Association. (2022). Infant vision: birth to 24 months of age. Accessed on July 20, 2022 through https://www.aoa.org/healthy-eyes/eye-health-for-life/infant-vision?sso=y
- Skoler, T. Ph.D. (2020). Color matters and child development. Accessed on July 20, 2022 through https://www.psychologytoday.com/us/blog/smart-baby/202009/color-matters-and-child-development
- Westland, S. (2017). Here's how colours really affect our brain and body, according to science. Accessed on July 20, 2022 through https://www.sciencealert.com/does-colour-really-affect-our-brain-and-body-a-professor-of-colour-science-explains
- Cleveland Clinic. (2022). Pituitary gland. Accessed on July 20, 2022 through https://my.clevelandclinic.org/health/body/21459-pituitary-gland
- Cleveland Clinic. (2022). Hypothalamus. Accessed on July 20, 2022 through https://my.clevelandclinic.org/health/articles/22566-hypothalamus
- Richardson, M. (2018). Rods and cones. Accessed on July 20, 2022 through https://www.brainfacts.org/thinking-sensing-and-behaving/vision/2018/rods-and-cones-061518
- Van Braam, H. (2022). How the eyes and brain process color. Accessed on July 20, 2022 through https://www.colorpsychology.org/how-the-eyes-and-brain-process-color/

- Kay, P. PNAS (2011). Learning new color names produces rapid increase in gray matter in the intact adult human cortex. Accessed on July 20, 2022 through https://www.p-nas.org/doi/full/10.1073/pnas.1103217108
- Bird, C. Berens, S. Horner, A. Franklin, A. Edited by Kay, P. Stanford University. (2014). Categorical encoding of color in the brain. Accessed on July 20, 2022 through https://www.p-nas.org/doi/10.1073/pnas.1315275111
- Li, Q. Kobayashi, M. Wakayama, Y. Inagaki, H. Katsumata, M. Hirata, Y. Hirata, K. Shimizu, T. Kawada, T. Park, B. Ohira, T. Kagawa, T. Miyazaki, Y. (2009). Effect of phytoncide from trees on human natural killer cell function. Accessed on July 21, 2022 through https://pubmed.ncbi.nlm.nih.gov/20074458/

Color Physics

- Encyclopedia Britannica. (2022). Learn about Thomas Young's double-slit experiment which contradicted Newton's theory of light. Accessed on July 19, 2022 through https://www.britanni-ca.com/video/179685/experiment-Thomas-Young
- Kotsche, Charles. Color Medicine. Light Technology Publishing, 1992.
- Wikipedia contributors. (2021, April 6). Observer effect. In *Wikipedia, The Free Encyclopedia*. Retrieved 01:38, July 21, 2022, from https://en.wikipedia.org/w/index.php?title=Observer_effect&oldid=1016278514
- Nobel Lectures, Physics 1922-1941, Elsevier Publishing Company, Amsterdam. (1965). Accessed on July 19, 2022 through https://www.nobel-prize.org/prizes/physics/1929/broglie/biographical
- Cline, B. Encyclopedia Britannica. (2022). Louis de Broglie. Accessed on July 19, 2022 through https://www.britannica.-com/biography/Louis-de-Broglie

- Plante, A. University of Maryland Graduate School. (2016) How the human body uses electricity. Accessed on July 19, 2022 through https://www.graduate.umaryland.edu/gsa/gazette/February-2016/How-the-human-body-uses-electricity/

- Pawluk, W. M.D. M.Sc. (2021). Biomagnetic fields and the human body. Accessed on July 19, 2022 through https://www.dr-pawluk.com/education/magnetic-science/biomagnetic-fields

- Sundermier, A. U.S. Department of Energy. (2015). The particle physics of you. Accessed on July 19, 2022 through https://www.energy.gov/articles/particle-physics-you

- London Image Institute. (2020). How much of communication is nonverbal? Accessed on July 19, 2022 through https://london-imageinstitute.com/how-much-of-communication-is-nonverbal/

RED

- Haller, Karen. The Little Book Of Color. Penguin Random House UK, 2019.

- Kotsche, Charles. Color Medicine. Light Technology Publishing, 1992.

- Bellantoni, Patti. If It's Purple, Someone's Gunna Die. Focal Press, 2005.

- Brent A. Bauer, MD. (2022). What is an infrared sauna? Does it have health benefits? Accessed July 18, 2022 through https://www.mayoclinic.org/healthy-lifestyle/consumer-health/expert-answers/infrared-sauna/faq-20057954

- Melissa Young, MD. (2022). Infrared saunas: what they do and 6 health benefits. Accessed July 18,2022 through https://health.clevelandclinic.org/infrared-sauna-benefits/

- Ernst, E. Pecho, E. Wirz, P. Saradeth, T. (2009). Regular sauna bathing and the incidence of common colds. Accessed July 18,2022 through https://pubmed.ncbi.nlm.nih.gov/2248758/

- Sunlighten Inc (2022). Clinical Research. Accessed July 18, 2022 through https://www.sunlighten.com/light-science/research

- Lubos, Leslie C. (2008). The role of colors in stress reduction. Accessed July 19, 2022 through https://www.research-gate.net/publication/314578015_The_Role_of_Colors_in_Stress_Reduction

- Elliot, A. Niesta, D. via University of Rochester 'Journal of Personality and Social Psychology' (2008.) Psychological study reveals that red enhances men's attraction to women. Accessed July 19, 2022 through https://www.rochester.edu/news/show.php?id=3268

- Wikipedia contributors. (2022, July 19). Red. In *Wikipedia, The Free Encyclopedia*. Retrieved 02:38, July 20, 2022, through https://en.wikipedia.org/w/index.php?title=Red&oldid=1099162355

- Martinez-Conde, S. Macknik, S. (2014). How the color red influences our behavior. Accessed July 19, 2022 through https://www.scientificamerican.com/article/how-the-color-red-influences-our-behavior/

- Kuniecki, M. Pilarczyk, J. Wichary, S. (2015). The color red attracts attention in an emotional context. An ERP study. Accessed July 19, 2022 through https://www.frontiersin.org/articles/10.3389/fnhum.2015.00212/full

- University of Rochester. (2007). Research on the color red shows definite impact on achievement. Accessed July 19, 2022 through https://www.sciencedaily.com/releases/2007/02/070228170240.htm

- Dr. Watrelot, A. (2020). Pigments in grapes - anthocyanins. Accessed July 19, 2022 through https://www.extension.iastate.e-

du/wine/focusing-research-winemaking-pigments-grapes-
anthocyanins/

- Lavender, N. (2019). Scientists have just discovered what really
  causes red hair. Accessed July 19, 2022 through
  https://www.brit.co/study-explains-red-hair/
- Stewart, S. (2021). Color meanings in different cultures.
  Accessed July 19, 2022 through https://study.com/acad-
  emy/lesson/color-meanings-in-different-cultures.html
- Wikipedia contributors. (2022, June 22). Pan-African colours.
  In *Wikipedia, The Free Encyclopedia*. Retrieved 02:47, July 20,
  2022, through https://en.wikipedia.org/w/index.php?title=Pan-
  African_colours&oldid=1094399385
- Donnella, L. (2017). On Flag Day, remembering the red, black
  and green. Accessed July 19, 2022 through https://www.n-
  pr.org/sections/codeswitch/2017/06/14/532667081/on-flag-day-
  remembering-the-red-black-and-green
- Kubilius, K. (2019). The significance of the color red in Russian
  culture. Accessed July 20, 2022 through
  https://www.thoughtco.com/red-in-russian-culture-1502319
- Olsen, J. (2013) What is the opposite of red? Accessed July 20,
  2022 through https://www.color-meanings.com/what-is-the-
  opposite-of-red/
- Bass-Kreuger, M. (2022). The secret history of the color red.
  Accessed July 30, 2022 through https://artsandculture.google.-
  com/story/the-secret-history-of-the-color-red
- Mellor, M. (2022). A brief history of the colour red. Accessed July
  30, 2022 through https://www.artsandcollections.com/article/a-
  history-of-the-colour-red
- Wikipedia contributors. (2022, January 28). Kermes (dye).
  In *Wikipedia, The Free Encyclopedia*. Retrieved 22:01, July 30,
  2022, from https://en.wikipedia.org/w/index.php?
  title=Kermes_(dye)&oldid=1068388451

- Azeemi ST, Raza SM. A critical analysis of chromotherapy and its scientific evolution. Evid Based Complement Alternat Med. 2005 Dec;2(4):481-8. doi: 10.1093/ecam/neh137. PMID: 16322805; PMCID: PMC1297510.
- Wikipedia contributors. (2022, July 27). Avicenna. In *Wikipedia, The Free Encyclopedia*. Retrieved 03:10, August 1, 2022, from https://en.wikipedia.org/w/index.php?title=Avicenna&oldid=1100830770
- Wikipedia contributors. (2022, July 22). The Book of Healing. In *Wikipedia, The Free Encyclopedia*. Retrieved 03:11, August 1, 2022, from https://en.wikipedia.org/w/index.php?title=The_Book_of_Healing&oldid=1099689035
- Bioregulatory Medicine Institute. (2022). Bioregulatory medicine. Accessed on July 31, 2022 through https://www.bio-logicalmedicineinstitute.com/edwin-dwight-babbitt
- Rosewell Park Comprehensive Cancer Center. (2021). Thomas Dougherty, PhD: pioneer of photodynamic therapy. Accessed July 31, 2022 through https://cancerhistoryproject.com/people/thomas-dougherty-phd-pioneer-of-photodynamic-therapy
- Politzer, B. (2010). Personal profile: let there be light - Dr. Thomas Dougherty and Photodynamic Therapy. Accessed July 31, 2022 through https://doi.org/10.1089/lms.1988.6.5.11
- Babbitt E. Principles of Light and Colour. MT, USA: Kessinger Publishing; 1942.

ORANGE

- Haller, Karen. The Little Book Of Color. Penguin Random House UK, 2019.
- Kotsche, Charles. Color Medicine. Light Technology Publishing, 1992.

- Bellantoni, Patti. If It's Purple, Someone's Gunna Die. Focal Press, 2005.
- Goldhirst, Noah. The Power Of Colors. EBook Pro Publishing, 2019.
- Association for Psychological Science. (2008). How carrots help us see the color orange. Accessed July 20, 2022 through https://www.sciencedaily.com/releases/2008/07/080722102723.htm
- Lena, Young Naturalistic Awards. (2019). A behavioral test to examine the evolution of color vision in vertebrates. Accessed July 20, 2022 through https://www.amnh.org/learn-teach/curriculum-collections/young-naturalist-awards/winning-essays/2009/a-behavioral-test-to-examine-the-evolution-of-color-vision-in-vertebrates
- Douma, M. Lipscher, J. (2022). Short history of orange pigments. Accessed July 20, 2022 through http://www.webexhibits.org/pigments/intro/oranges.html
- BBC News. (2022). Mark Rothko work sold for a record $86.9 million at auction. Accessed July 20, 2022 through https://www.bbc.com/news/world-us-canada-18001432
- Phillips, K. (2021). The color orange - history, meanings and facts. Accessed July 20, 2022 through https://blog.hunterlab.com/blog/color-and-appearance-theory/the-color-orange
- Wikipedia contributors. (2022, July 19). Orange (colour). In *Wikipedia, The Free Encyclopedia*. Retrieved 22:08, July 20, 2022, from https://en.wikipedia.org/w/index.php?title=Orange_(colour)&oldid=1099131950
- Food Crumbles. (2016). Why is an orange, orange? Accessed July 20, 2022 through https://foodcrumbles.com/why-an-orange-is-orange/
- Explored Planet. (2022) Things on this planet aren't as natural as you think. Accessed July 20, 2022 through https://www.ex-

ploredplanet.com/info/things-on-this-planet-that-arent-as-natural-as-youd-think/?view-all&chrome=1

- Dutch Amersterdam. (2021) Why the Dutch wear orange. Accessed July 20, 2022 through https://www.dutchamsterdam.nl/321-why-the-dutch-wear-orange

- Olesen, J. (2013). Color meanings in India: find out what colors symbolize in Indian culture. Accessed July 20, 2022 through https://www.color-meanings.com/color-meanings-indian-culture/

- Yurka, B. (2014). Study findings suggest orange light causes people to be more alert. Accessed July 20, 2022 through https://medicalxpress.com/news/2014-03-orange-people.html

- Chellappa, S.L., Ly, J.Q.M., Meyer, C., Balteau, E., Degueldre, C., Luxen, A., Phillips, C., Cooper, H.M. and Vandewalle, G. (2014). Photic memory for executive brain responses. *PNAS* (In press): 1320005111v1-201320005. Published online ahead of print 10 March 2014. www.pnas.org/content/early/2014/03/07/1320005111.abstract

- Cynthia C. Chernecky PhD, RN, CNS, AOCN, FAAN, in Laboratory Tests and Diagnostic Procedures. (2013). Carotene. Accessed July 20, 2022 through https://www.sciencedirect.com/topics/medicine-and-dentistry/carotene

- Alkoziv, H. Department of Biochemistry, Faculty of Optics and Optometry, University Complutense, Madrid, Spain. (2019). Melatonin and melanopsin in the eye: friends or foes? Accessed July 21, 2022 through https://analesranf.com/articulo/8501_rev02/

- Han, X. Gibson, J. Eggett, D. Parker, T. National Library of Medicine. (2017). Bergamot (Citrus bergamia) essential oil inhalation improves positive feelings in the waitin groom of a mental health treatment center: a pilot study. Accessed July 21, 2022 through https://www.ncbi.nlm.nih.gov/pmc/articles/PMC5434918/

- Azeemi ST, Raza SM. A critical analysis of chromotherapy and its scientific evolution. Evid Based Complement Alternat Med. 2005 Dec;2(4):481-8. doi: 10.1093/ecam/neh137. PMID: 16322805; PMCID: PMC1297510.
- Live Science Staff. (2010). Chickens see color better than humans. Accessed August 2, 2022 through https://www.livescience.com/8099-chickens-color-humans.html
- Mellor, M. (2022). A history of the color orange. Accessed August 2, 2022 through https://www.artsandcollections.com/article/a-history-of-the-colour-orange

YELLOW

- Haller, Karen. The Little Book Of Color. Penguin Random House UK, 2019.
- Kotsche, Charles. Color Medicine. Light Technology Publishing, 1992.
- Bellantoni, Patti. If It's Purple, Someone's Gunna Die. Focal Press, 2005.
- Goldhirst, Noah. The Power Of Colors. EBook Pro Publishing, 2019.
- Wikipedia contributors. (2022, July 20). Yellow. In *Wikipedia, The Free Encyclopedia*. Retrieved 21:22, July 21, 2022, from https://en.wikipedia.org/w/index.php?title=Yellow&oldid=1099372783
- Kuhbandner, C. Spitzer, B. Lichtenfeld, S. Pekrun, R. (2015). Differential binding of colors to objects in memory: red and yellow stick better than blue and green. Accessed July 21, 2022 through https://www.frontiersin.org/articles/10.3389/fpsyg.2015.00231/full

- Kurt, S. Osueke, K. (2014). The effects of color on the moods of college students. Accessed on July 21, 2022 through https://journals.sagepub.com/doi/full/10.1177/2158244014525423

- Pastoureau, M. Yellow: The History Of A Color. Princeton Press, 2019.

- Mellor, M. (2022). A brief history of the colour yellow. Accessed July 21, 2022 through https://www.artsandcollections.com/article/a-history-of-the-colour-yellow/

- Rock Content Writer. (2011) The use of yellow in data design. Accessed on June 12, 2022 through https://rockcontent.com/blog/the-use-of-yellow-in-data-design/

- Danilenko KV, Ivanova IA. Dawn simulation vs. bright light in seasonal affective disorder: Treatment effects and subjective preference. J Affect Disord. 2015 Jul 15;180:87-9. doi: 10.1016/j.jad.2015.03.055. Epub 2015 Apr 7. PMID: 25885065.

- Gabel V, Maire M, Reichert CF, Chellappa SL, Schmidt C, Hommes V, Viola AU, Cajochen C. Effects of artificial dawn and morning blue light on daytime cognitive performance, well-being, cortisol and melatonin levels. Chronobiol Int. 2013 Oct;30(8):988-97. doi: 10.3109/07420528.2013.793196. Epub 2013 Jul 10. PMID: 23841684.

- Azeemi ST, Raza SM. A critical analysis of chromotherapy and its scientific evolution. Evid Based Complement Alternat Med. 2005 Dec;2(4):481-8. doi: 10.1093/ecam/neh137. PMID: 16322805; PMCID: PMC1297510.

- Coclivo A. Coloured light therapy: overview of its history, theory, recent developments and clinical applications combined with acupuncture. Am J Acupunct. 1999;27:71–83.

- Graham H. Discover Colour therapy. (2004) Ca USA: Ulysses Press; 1998.

- Perry R. Scientific documentation on colour therapy. Accessed July 31, 2022 at http://www.rachelperry.net/SCIENTIFIC.html.

GREEN

- Taggart, E. (2020). The history of the color green: from a poisonous pigment to a symbol of environmentalism. Accessed July 21, 2022 through https://mymodernmet.com/history-of-the-color-green/
- Haller, Karen. The Little Book Of Color. Penguin Random House UK, 2019.
- Kotsche, Charles. Color Medicine. Light Technology Publishing, 1992.
- Bellantoni, Patti. If It's Purple, Someone's Gunna Die. Focal Press, 2005.
- Goldhirst, Noah. The Power Of Colors. EBook Pro Publishing, 2019.
- Tompkins, Peter. Bird, Christopher. The Secret Life Of Plants. Harp & Row, Publishers, 1989.
- Wikipedia contributors. (2022, June 24). Green. In *Wikipedia, The Free Encyclopedia*. Retrieved 00:26, July 22, 2022, from https://en.wikipedia.org/w/index.php?title=Green&oldid=1094691191
- Hellem, A. Reviewed by Heiting, G. OD. (2019) Green eyes: the most attractive eye color? Accessed July 19, 2022 through https://www.allaboutvision.com/conditions/eye-color-green.htm
- Mellor, M. (2022). A history of the colour green. Accessed July 21, 2022 through https://www.artsandcollections.com/article/a-history-of-the-colour-green/
- Goldstein, J. Davidoff, J. Roberson, D. Journal of Experimental Child Psychology. (2008). Accessed on July 22, 2022 through https://research.gold.ac.uk/id/eprint/4935/1/davidoff-goldstein-color-terms.pdf

- Board Vitals. (2019). Why are scrubs usually green or blue? Accessed July 22, 2022 through https://www.boardvitals.com/blog/why-scrubs-usually-blue-green/

- Locke, S. (2013). Why do doctors wear green or blue scrubs? Accessed July 22, 2022 through https://www.livescience.com/32450-why-do-doctors-wear-green-or-blue-scrubs-.html

- Briki, W. Majed, L. National Library of Medicine. (2019). Adaptive effects of seeing green environment on psychophysiological parameters when walking or running. Accessed on July 22, 2022 through https://www.ncbi.nlm.nih.gov/pmc/articles/PMC6379348/

- Toselli, S. Bragonzoni, L. Dallolio, L. Alessia, G. Masini, A. Marini, S. Barone, G. Pinelli, E. Zinno, R. Mauro, M. Astorino, G. Pilone, P. Galli, S. Latessa, P. National Library of Medicine. (2019). The effects of park-based interventions on health: the Italian project "moving parks". Accessed on July 22, 2022 through https://pubmed.ncbi.nlm.nih.gov/35206319/

- Pei-Jou Kuo, Lu Zhang. (2021) The Impact of Hotel Room Colors on Affective Responses, Attitude, and Booking Intention. Accessed July 22, 2022 through https://www.tandfonline.com/doi/full/10.1080/13683500.2016.1217830

- Gladwell VF, Brown DK, Wood C, Sandercock GR, Barton JL. The great outdoors: how a green exercise environment can benefit all. Extrem Physiol Med. 2013 Jan 3;2(1):3. doi: 10.1186/2046-7648-2-3. PMID: 23849478; PMCID: PMC3710158.

- Fleming, A. (2020). The secret life of plants: how they memorize, communicate, problem solve and socialize. Accessed July 22, 2022 through https://www.theguardian.com/environment/2020/apr/05/smarty-plants-are-our-vegetable-cousins-more-intelligent-than-we-realise

- Chamovitz, Daniel. *What a Plant Knows: A Field Guide to the Senses.* New York: Scientific American/Farrar, Straus and Giroux, 2012.

- Wang, T. Harvard Science Review. (2014). The secret life of plants. Accessed on July 22, 2022 through https://harvard-sciencereview.org/2014/01/22/the-secret-life-of-plants/

- Sequoia Group. (2020.) The Sequoia Story. Accessed on July 22, 2022 through https://www.sequoia.com.sg/about-us/the-sequoia-story/

- Geeraert, A. (2020). Traditional meanings of colors in Japan. Accessed July 22, 2022 through https://kokoro-jp.com/culture/298/

- Oleson, J. (2020). Color meanings in Japan. Accessed July 22, 2022 through https://www.color-meanings.com/color-meanings-japan/

- Oleson, J. (2020). Native American Color Meanings. Accessed July 22, 2022 through https://www.color-meanings.com/native-american-color-meanings/

- Waxman, O. (2020). How green became associated with St. Patrick's Day and all things Irish. Accessed July 22, 2022 through https://time.com/4699771/green-irish-st-patricks-day-color/

- Irish Music Daily. (2020). Wearing of the green - symbol of Irish nationalism. Accessed July 22, 2022 through https://www.irish-musicdaily.com/wearing-of-the-green

- AZIslam. (2022). 13 importance of green color in Islamic perspective. Accessed on July 22, 2022 through https://azislam.-com/importance-of-green-color-in-islam

- Muslims Today. (2022). Is there any relation to green and the Prophet Muhammad? Accessed July 22, 2022 through https://azislam.com/importance-of-green-color-in-islam

- Chevalier G, Sinatra ST, Oschman JL, Sokal K, Sokal P. Earthing: health implications of reconnecting the human body to the Earth's surface electrons. J Environ Public Health.

2012;2012:291541. doi: 10.1155/2012/291541. Epub 2012 Jan 12. PMID: 22291721; PMCID: PMC3265077.

- Oschman JL, Chevalier G, Brown R. The effects of grounding (earthing) on inflammation, the immune response, wound healing, and prevention and treatment of chronic inflammatory and autoimmune diseases. J Inflamm Res. 2015 Mar 24;8:83-96. doi: 10.2147/JIR.S69656. PMID: 25848315; PMCID: PMC4378297.

- Azeemi ST, Raza SM. A critical analysis of chromotherapy and its scientific evolution. Evid Based Complement Alternat Med. 2005 Dec;2(4):481-8. doi: 10.1093/ecam/neh137. PMID: 16322805; PMCID: PMC1297510.

- Babbitt E. Principles of Light and Colour. MT, USA: Kessinger Publishing; 1942.

- Ghadiali D. Spectrochrome Metery Encyclopedia. NJ, USA: Dinshah Health Society; 1997.

BLUE

- Haller, Karen. The Little Book Of Color. Penguin Random House UK, 2019.

- Kotsche, Charles. Color Medicine. Light Technology Publishing, 1992.

- Bellantoni, Patti. If It's Purple, Someone's Gunna Die. Focal Press, 2005.

- Goldhirst, Noah. The Power Of Colors. EBook Pro Publishing, 2019.

- The Tiger Editorial Board. (2022). Blue light system on campus. Accessed July 24, 2022 through https://www.thetigercu.-com/outlook/editorial/editorial-blue-light-system-on-campus/article_b9198704-b5fd-11ec-a5ea-4faae2ba55d5.html

- Blue Light Emergency Phones. (2022). Accessed July 24, 2022 through https://www.caseemergencysystems.com/

- Matsubayashi, T. Sawada, Y. Ueda, M. (2014). Does the installation of blue lights on train platforms shift suicide to another station? Evidence from Japan. Journal of Affective Disorders, Volume 169, 2014, Pages 57-60, ISSN 0165-0327, https://doi.org/10.1016/j.jad.2014.07.036.
- Psych Central. (2008). Can blue-colored light prevent suicide? Accessed on July 24, 2022 through https://psychcentral.-com/blog/can-blue-colored-light-prevent-suicide#1
- Raphael Knaier, Juliane Schäfer, Anja Rossmeissl, Christopher Klenk, Henner Hanssen, Christoph Höchsmann, Christian Cajochen, and Arno Schmidt-Trucksäss
- Prime Time Light Exposures Do Not Seem to Improve Maximal Physical Performance in Male Elite Athletes, but Enhance End-Spurt Performance
- Frontiers in Physiology (2017), doi: 10.3389/fphys.2017.00264
- Vicente-Tejedor J, Marchena M, Ramírez L, García-Ayuso D, Gómez-Vicente V, Sánchez-Ramos C, et al. (2018) Removal of the blue component of light significantly decreases retinal damage after high intensity exposure. PLoS ONE 13(3): e0194218. https://doi.org/10.1371/journal.pone.0194218
- Wikipedia contributors. (2022, July 24). Blue. In *Wikipedia, The Free Encyclopedia*. Retrieved 20:52, July 24, 2022, from https://en.wikipedia.org/w/index.php?title=Blue&oldid=1100063502
- Wikipedia contributors. (2022, July 20). Aerial perspective. In *Wikipedia, The Free Encyclopedia*. Retrieved 20:52, July 24, 2022, from https://en.wikipedia.org/w/index.php?title=Aerial_perspective&oldid=1099346513
- Westland, S. (2017). Here's how colours really affect our brain and body, according to science. Accessed on July 24, 2022 through https://www.sciencealert.com/does-colour-really-affect-our-brain-and-body-a-professor-of-colour-science-explains

- Al-Ayash, A. Kane, R. Smith, D. Green-Armytage, P. (2015). The influence of color on student learning, heart rate and performance in learning environments. Accessed July 24, 2022 through https://doi.org/10.1002/col.21949
- Mangla, R. (2015). True blue. Accessed on July 24, 2022 through https://www.theparisreview.org/blog/2015/06/08/true-blue
- Taggart, E. (2018). The history of the color blue: from Ancient Egypt to the latest scientific discoveries. Accessed on July 24, 2022 through https://mymodernmet.com/shades-of-blue-color-history
- Weisburger, Mindy. (2021). Why is the color blue so rare in nature? Accessed on July 24, 2022 through https://www.live-science.com/why-blue-rare-in-nature.html
- Kupferschmidt, Kai. Blue: In Search Of Nature's Rarest Color. Hoffman and Campe Verlag, Hamburg, 2019.
- Professor Andy Rowe. (2019). Why is the colour blue so rare in nature? Accessed on July 24, 2022 through https://set.adelaide.e-du.au/news/list/2019/08/20/why-is-the-colour-blue-so-rare-in-nature
- McAwley, J. (2020). Blue symbolism in Hinduism. Accessed on July 24, 2022 through https://slightlyblue.com/culture/blue-symbolism-in-hinduism/
- *The Bible*. Christian Standard Version, Tony Evans, Holman Bible Publishers, 2017. Numbers 4:6-12.
- Erikson Translations. (2020). How translating colors across cultures can help you make a positive impact. Accessed July 24, 2022 through https://eriksen.com/marketing/color_culture
- Wikipedia contributors. (2022, July 4). Indigo dye. In *Wikipedia, The Free Encyclopedia*. Retrieved 01:20, July 27, 2022, from https://en.wikipedia.org/w/index.php?title=Indigo_dye&oldid=1096367201
- Azeemi ST, Raza SM. A critical analysis of chromotherapy and its scientific evolution. Evid Based Complement Alternat Med.

2005 Dec;2(4):481-8. doi: 10.1093/ecam/neh137. PMID: 16322805; PMCID: PMC1297510.

- Ebbesen F, Agati G, Pratesi R. Phototherapy with turquoise verses blue light. Archiv Des Childhood Fetal Neonatal Edn. 2003;88:F430.
- Azeemi, Khawaja Shamsuddin. Colour Therapy. Karachi: Al-Kitab Publications; 1999.
- Pleasanton A. Blue and Sun Light. Philadelphia: Claxton, Reuser & Haffelfinger; 1876.
- Babbitt E. Principles of Light and Colour. MT, USA: Kessinger Publishing; 1942.

PURPLE

- Haller, Karen. The Little Book Of Color. Penguin Random House UK, 2019.
- Kotsche, Charles. Color Medicine. Light Technology Publishing, 1992.
- Bellantoni, Patti. If It's Purple, Someone's Gunna Die. Focal Press, 2005.
- Goldhirst, Noah. The Power Of Colors. EBook Pro Publishing, 2019.
- Nature Collective. (2022). Accessed on July 25, 2022 through https://thenaturecollective.org/plant-guide/by-color/purple/
- Hendry, L. Dunning, H. (2022). Rainbow nature: life in majestic purple. Accessed on July 25, 2022 through https://www.nhm.ac.uk/discover/rainbow-nature-life-in-majestic-purple.html
- Wikipedia contributors. (2022, July 12). Purple. In *Wikipedia, The Free Encyclopedia*. Retrieved 20:37, July 25, 2022, from https://en.wikipedia.org/w/index.php?title=Purple&oldid=1097818052

- Wikipedia contributors. (2022, April 26). Tyrian purple. In *Wikipedia, The Free Encyclopedia*. Retrieved 22:05, July 27, 2022, from https://en.wikipedia.org/w/index.php?title=Tyrian_purple&oldid=1084845024

- Feng, Zhao, "Woven Color in China/ The Five Colors in Chinese Culture and Polychrome Woven Textiles" (2010). Textile Society of America Symposium Proceedings. 63. https://digitalcommons.unl.edu/tsaconf/63

- Oleson, J. (2013). Color symbolism in Chinese culture: what do traditional Chinese colors mean? Accessed on July 12, 2022 through https://www.color-meanings.com/color-symbolism-in-chinese-culture-what-do-traditional-chinese-colors-mean

- Varichon, Anne Colors: What They Mean and How to Make Them New York: 2006 Abrams Page 140 – This information is in the caption of a color illustration showing an 8th-century manuscript page of the Gospel of Luke written in gold on Tyrian purple parchment.

- History, Art & Archives: United States House Of Representatives. (2022). The Women's Rights Movement, 1848-1927. Accessed on July 12, 2022 through https://history.house.gov/Exhibitions-and-Publications/WIC/Historical-Essays/No-Lady/Womens-Rights

- Daydream Tourist. (2014). Caesar and the snail: "royal purple" in Imperial Rome. Accessed on July 12, 2022 through https://daydreamtourist.com/2014/10/06/roman-purple

- Wikipedia contributors. (2022, June 10). Purple triangle. In *Wikipedia, The Free Encyclopedia*. Retrieved 20:43, July 25, 2022, from https://en.wikipedia.org/w/index.php?title=Purple_-triangle&oldid=1092508725

- Elliott, C. (2008). Purple Pasts: Color Codification in the Ancient World. Accessed July 12, 2022 through https://www.jstor.org/stable/20108752?read-now=1&seq=1#page_scan_tab_contents

- Kelley, Tanya. "violet". *Encyclopedia Britannica*, 19 Sep. 2019, https://www.britannica.com/science/violet. Accessed 25 July 2022.

- Micu, A. (2021). The color purple is unlike all others, in a physical sense. Accessed on July 25, 2022 through https://www.zmescience.com/science/color-purple-non-spectral-feature

- Wikipedia contributors. (2022, February 19). Bezold–Brücke shift. In *Wikipedia, The Free Encyclopedia*. Retrieved 21:39, July 25, 2022, from https://en.wikipedia.org/w/index.php?title=Bezold%E2%80%93Br%C3%BC-cke_shift&oldid=1072883798

- Kaya, N. Ph. D. Epps, H. Ph. D. (2004). Relationship between color and emotion: a study of college students. Accessed on July 25, 2022 through https://www.academi-a.edu/3880952/RELATIONSHIP_BETWEEN_COLOR_AND_E-MOTION_A_STUDY_OF_COLLEGE_STUDENTS

- Cousins, C. (2012). Color and cultural design considerations. Accessed July 24, 2022 through https://www.webdesignerde-pot.com/2012/06/color-and-cultural-design-considerations

- Foskett, H. (2022). A history of the colour purple. Accessed July 25, 2022 through https://www.artsandcollections.com/a-history-of-the-colour-purple

- McClelland MM, Tominey SL, Schmitt SA, Hatfield BE, Purpura DJ, Gonzales CR and Tracy AN (2019) Red Light, Purple Light! Results of an Intervention to Promote School Readiness for Children From Low-Income Backgrounds. *Front. Psychol.* 10:2365. doi: 10.3389/fpsyg.2019.02365

- Ciotti, G. (2014). Color psychology: how colors influence the mind. Accessed on July 25, 2022 through https://www.psycholo-gytoday.com/us/blog/habits-not-hacks/201408/color-psychology-how-colors-influence-the-mind

- Cavenagh, R. Thaizer. (2022). HRH Princess Maha Chakri Sirindhorn. Accessed July 25, 2022 through https://www.thaizer.com/hrh-princess-maha-chakri-sirindhorn
- Wikipedia contributors. (2022, July 14). Colors of the day in Thailand. In *Wikipedia, The Free Encyclopedia*. Retrieved 23:09, July 25, 2022, from https://en.wikipedia.org/w/index.php?title=Colors_of_the_day_in_Thailand&oldid=1098177299
- DeSimone, D. (2021). 8 things you need to know about the Purple Heart Metal. Accessed July 25, 2022 through https://www.uso.org/stories/2276-8-purple-heart-facts
- Funeral Guide. (2017). Colours of mourning around the world. Accessed July 25, 2022 through https://www.funeral-guide.net/blog/mourning-colours
- Azeemi ST, Raza SM. A critical analysis of chromotherapy and its scientific evolution. Evid Based Complement Alternat Med. 2005 Dec;2(4):481-8. doi: 10.1093/ecam/neh137. PMID: 16322805; PMCID: PMC1297510.
- Kortkov K. Accessed July 31, 2022 through http://www.kirlianresearch.com

PINK

- Haller, Karen. The Little Book Of Color. Penguin Random House UK, 2019.
- Kotsche, Charles. Color Medicine. Light Technology Publishing, 1992.
- Bellantoni, Patti. If It's Purple, Someone's Gunna Die. Focal Press, 2005.
- Goldhirst, Noah. The Power Of Colors. EBook Pro Publishing, 2019.

- O'Dea, S. (2022). T-Mobile US statistics & facts. Accessed July 26, 2022 through https://www.statista.com/topics/996/t-mobile-us/#dossierKeyfigures

- T-Mobile. (2020). T-Mobile overtakes AT&T as America's #2 wireless provider and continues to deliver industry-leading customer growth with strong financial results in Q2 2020. Accessed July 26, 2022 through https://www.t-mobile.com/news/un-carrier/t-mobile-q2-2020-earnings

- Lewis, D. (2014). The case of the missing magenta. Accessed July 26, 2022 through https://nowiknow.com/the-case-of-the-missing-magenta

- Oddity Central. (2021). The Pink Panthers - a unique piece of British military history. Accessed July 26, 2022 through https://www.odditycentral.com/auto/the-pink-panthers-a-unique-piece-of-british-military-history.html

- Nisa, Janet. (2021). Meet the Pink Panthers - a unique remnant of the British Army's history. Accessed July 26, 2022 through https://wonderfulengineering.com/meet-the-pink-panthers-a-unique-remnant-of-the-british-army-during-ww2

- Wikipedia contributors. (2022, June 24). Land Rover series. In *Wikipedia, The Free Encyclopedia*. Retrieved 21:11, July 26, 2022, from https://en.wikipedia.org/w/index.php?title=Land_Rover_series&oldid=1094790585

- Wikipedia contributors. (2022, July 24). Louis Mountbatten, 1st Earl Mountbatten of Burma. In *Wikipedia, The Free Encyclopedia*. Retrieved 21:11, July 26, 2022, from https://en.wikipedi-a.org/w/index.php?title=Louis_Mountbatten,_1st_Earl_Mount-batten_of_Burma&oldid=1100128822

- Wikipedia contributors. (2021, December 29). Mountbatten pink. In *Wikipedia, The Free Encyclopedia*. Retrieved 21:11, July 26, 2022, from https://en.wikipedia.org/w/index.php?title=Mountbatten_pink&oldid=1062622247

- Wikipedia contributors. (2022, July 26). Pink. In *Wikipedia, The Free Encyclopedia*. Retrieved 22:03, July 26, 2022, from https://en.wikipedia.org/w/index.php? title=Pink&oldid=1100611647

- Mauney, A. (2022). The color pink: a cultural history. Accessed July 26, 2022 through https://www.artandobject.-com/news/color-pink-cultural-history

- Smithsonian. (1984). Rock Against Reagan. Accessed July 26, 2022 through https://www.si.edu/object/rock-against-reagan-tank-top%3Anmah_1899166

- Wikipedia contributors. (2022, July 7). Magenta. In *Wikipedia, The Free Encyclopedia*. Retrieved 22:44, July 26, 2022, from https://en.wikipedia.org/w/index.php? title=Magenta&oldid=1096935642

- Royal Talens. (2022). Magenta: a colour with a bloody past. Accessed July 26, 2022 through https://www.royaltalens.-com/en/inspiration/tips-techniques/colour-stories/magenta-a-colour-with-a-bloody-past

- Smith, Kate. (2022). What's behind the colour name Magenta. Accessed July 26, 2022 through https://www.sensationalcol-or.com/origin-of-the-word-magenta

- Horowitz, J. Vogue. (2018). How Pope Francis is changing the Catholic church. Accessed July 26, 2022 through https://www.vogue.com/article/pope-francis-vogue-august-2018-issue

- Camosy, C. (2013). Pope Francis, the Magenta Catholic. Accessed on July 26, 2022 through https://onbeing.org/blog/pope-francis-the-magenta-catholic

- Schauss, Alexander. (1985). The Physiological Effect of Color on the Suppression of Human Aggression: Research on Baker-Miller Pink. International Journal of Biosocial Research. 7. 55-64.

- Daley, B. (2018). Can pink really pacify? Accessed July 26, 2022 through https://theconversation.com/can-pink-really-pacify-102696

- Daniela SPÄTH, Dipl. Farbdesignerin ICA, Color Motion GmbH. Der psychologische und physiologische Effekt von "Cool Down Pink" auf das menschliche Verhalten. Accessed July 26, 2022 through http://www.colormotion.ch/download/cool-down-pink/wissenschaftlicher-Kurzbericht-Cool-Down-Pink.pdf

- Schauss, A. (1979). Tranquilizing Effect of Color Reduces Aggressive Behavior and Potential Violence. Accessed July 26, 2022 through https://isom.ca/wp-content/uploads/2020/01/JOM_1979_08_4_01_Tranquilizing_Effect_of_Color_Reduces_Aggressive-.pdf

- Man, J. (2022). This colour has an actual superpower. Accessed July 26, 2022 through https://brainfodder.org/drunk-tank-pink

- Adam, K. (2018). Glasgow was once 'the murder capital of Europe'. Now it's a model for cutting crime. Accessed July 26, 2022 through https://www.washingtonpost.com/world/europe/glasgow-was-once-the-murder-capital-of-europe-now-its-a-model-for-cutting-crime/2018/10/27/0b167e68-6e02-4795-92f8-adb1020b7434_story.html

- Wikipedia contributors. (2022, June 3). Battle of Magenta. In *Wikipedia, The Free Encyclopedia*. Retrieved 00:51, July 27, 2022, from https://en.wikipedia.org/w/index.php?title=Battle_of_Magenta&oldid=1091383728

- Gulabi Gang. (2022). Accessed July 30, 3033 through https://gulabigang.in

- Kay Brown. Four 4 Consent. www.four4consent.org

EATING COLOR

- Ganora, L. Herbal Constituents: Foundations of Phytochemistry. (2009).

THE LIGHTS IN YOUR HOME - HELPFUL OR HURTFUL?

- American Cancer Society. (2022). Ultraviolet (UV) radiation. Accessed July 31, 2022 through https://www.cancer.org/healthy/cancer-causes/radiation-exposure/uv-radiation.html
- Prakash, M. (2017). Exposure to LED lights could be harmful; scientists suggest a simple solution. Accessed July 31, 2022 through https://www.downtoearth.org.in/news/environment/exposure-to-led-lights-could-be-harmful-scientists-suggest-a-simple-solution-58544
- Make Light Great. (2020). The critical distinctions between full-spectrum bulbs and daylight bulbs. Accessed July 31, 2022 through https://www.makegreatlight.com/about-us/blog/difference-between-full-spectrum-bulbs-daylight-bulbs
- Zhao, Z. Zhou, Y. Tan, G. Li, J. (2018). Research progress about the effect and prevention of blue light on eyes. Accessed on July 31, 2022 through https://www.ncbi.nlm.nih.gov/pmc/articles/PMC6288536
- Statista. (2022). Leading restaurant brands worldwide in 2022, by brand value. Accessed July 31, 2022 through https://www.statista.com/statistics/407892/brand-value-of-the-leading-global-fast-food-brands/
- Lamp HQ. (2022). What is color rendering index (CRI) for LED lights? Accessed August 3, 2022 through

https://lamphq.com/color-rendering-index/

ARE YOU ALREADY BEING MANIPULATED BY COLOR?

- Urie, C. (2018). There's a sneaky reason why you always see red and yellow on fast food logos. Accessed on July 30, 2022 through https://www.insider.com/fast-food-colors-make-you-hungry-2018-9
- I Spot TV. (2022). McDonalds commercial. Accessed July 31, 2022 through https://www.ispot.tv/ad/q8Ge/mcdonalds-the-now-im-a-morning-person-deal-sausage-mcmuffin-with-egg-and-sausage-egg-and-cheese-mc
- Salakay, K. (2019). Here's why so many fast food logos are red and yellow. Accessed on July 30, 2022 through https://www.del-ish.com/food/a29490183/why-are-fast-food-logos-red/
- Taco Bell (2022). Http://tacobell.com

WHY RED & BLUE TIES WIN PRESIDENCIES

- Journal of the Society of Dyers and Colourists. (2000). Healing Colour. 116(9): 257-259. Accessed August 3, 2022 through https://www.research-gate.net/publication/296015259_Healing_colour
- Lang, C. TIME. (2020). Why democratic Congresswomen wore white again to send a message at the State of the Union. Accessed August 3, 2022 through https://time.-com/5777514/women-wearing-white-state-of-the-union
- Moniuszko, S. USA Today. (2021). Why is everyone wearing purple during Inauguration week? Accessed August 3, 2022 through https://www.usatoday.com/story/life/fash-

ion/2021/01/20/inauguration-why-kamala-harris-jill-biden-wearing-purple/4229427001

- Erb. K. Forbes. (2016). Live blog: the Republican Presidential debate. Accessed August 3, 2022 through https://www.forbes.-com/sites/kellyphillipserb/2016/02/13/live-blog-the-republican-presidential-debate-february-13-2016/?sh=373b90ca2d36

- Peralta, E. NPR. (2016). The 10th Republican debate in 100 words. Accessed August 3, 2022 through https://www.n-pr.org/sections/thetwo-way/2016/02/25/468199314/the-10th-republican-debate-in-100-words-and-3-videos

- Collinson, S. CNN. (2017). Clinton puts Trump on defense at first debate. Accessed August 3, 2022 through https://www.cnn.-com/2016/09/26/politics/presidential-debate-hillary-clinton-donald-trump

- Breuninger, K. CNBC. (2020). Here are the key moments from the final Trump-Biden Presidential Debate. Accessed August 3, 2022 through https://www.cnbc.com/2020/10/22/final-presidential-debate-highlights-trump-vs-biden.html

- Lapakko, D. Department of Communication Studies Augsburg College Minneapolis, MN. (2007). Communication is 93% Nonverbal: An Urban Legend Proliferates. Accessed July 30, 2022. https://cornerstone.lib.mnsu.edu/cgi/viewcontent.cgi?article=1000&context=ctamj

www.ingramcontent.com/pod-product-compliance
Lightning Source LLC
Chambersburg PA
CBHW062130020426

42335CB00013B/1167